THE GLOBAL FREELANCER

In *The Global Freelancer*, award-winning journalist Steve Dorsey draws on his own experiences, as well as those of fellow reporters and editors, to instruct aspiring freelancers on all aspects of becoming a foreign correspondent. Topics covered include: delivering successful story pitches, location scouting, navigating foreign work documentation and visa requirements, confronting press freedom restrictions, leveraging digital media opportunities, and the new challenges of reporting from conflict zones safely.

As newspapers and networks are forced to close their overseas bureaus, news organizations are relying more than ever before on freelancers to fill the gap. This book offers the freelance foreign correspondents of tomorrow step-by-step guidance on how to seize these opportunities and make a name in this competitive field. Packed with practical guidance, tips, and anecdotes from working professionals, *The Global Freelancer* is your gateway to a career in foreign journalism.

Steve Dorsey is the Executive Editor/Correspondent for Radio at CBS News based in the Washington Bureau. Dorsey has been a longtime award-winning freelance journalist, reporting from Turkey, Russia, Spain, Australia, and New Zealand for major media organizations including CBS News, CNN.com, Voice of America, NPR, CBC, and Bloomberg BNA. He has also worked as a producer for FOX News—covering everything from Congress to The White House and is an advocate for freelance journalists, and mentors young reporters and journalism students.

THE GLOBAL FREELANCER

Telling and Selling Foreign News

Steve Dorsey

Routledge
Taylor & Francis Group

NEW YORK AND LONDON

First published 2017
by Routledge
711 Third Avenue, New York, NY 10017

and by Routledge
2 Park Square, Milton Park, Abingdon, Oxon OX14 4RN

Routledge is an imprint of the Taylor & Francis Group, an informa business

© 2017 Taylor & Francis

Library of Congress Cataloging-in-Publication Data
Names: Dorsey, Steve, author.
Title: The global freelancer : telling & selling foreign news / Steve Dorsey.
Description: Milton Park, Abingdon, Oxon ; New York, NY : Routledge, 2016. |
    Includes bibliographical references.
Identifiers: LCCN 2015050554 | ISBN 9781138101562 (hardback) |
    ISBN 9781138999787 (pbk.)
Subjects: LCSH: Journalism—Vocational guidance—United States. | Reporters
    and reporting—Vocational guidance. | Foreign news—United States.
Classification: LCC PN4888.F69 D67 2016 | DDC 071/.3023—dc23
LC record available at http://lccn.loc.gov/2015050554

ISBN: 978-1-138-10156-2 (hbk)
ISBN: 978-1-138-99978-7 (pbk)
ISBN: 978-1-315-65794-3 (ebk)

Typeset in Bembo
by Apex CoVantage, LLC

Printed and bound in the United States of America by Publishers Graphics,
LLC on sustainably sourced paper.

To My Parents, Ron and Maria, Who Always Supported My Dreams

CONTENTS

PREFACE

The last two decades have brought seismic shifts in foreign newsgathering and correspondence. At least 18 newspapers and two chains have shuttered all their overseas bureaus since 1998.[1] One of the most recent casualties in foreign newsgathering for newspapers is the shuttering in 2015 of the McClatchy Company's remaining five foreign bureaus that had produced exceptional reporting for its 30 U.S. newspapers.[2] The decision to close the celebrated foreign bureaus left just a handful of big U.S. newspapers such as the *New York Times*, the *Wall Street Journal* and the *Washington Post* with a regular independent foreign editorial presence.

American TV networks each maintained about 15 foreign bureaus in the 1980s, while these days they have fewer than six.[3] The amount of coverage with foreign datelines on the big three network evening newscasts in the U.S. in 2013 was less than half of what it was in late 1980s, according to Andrew Tyndall who tracks and logs the broadcasts.[4]

Even at the iconic BBC, hundreds of layoffs and budget cuts have chiseled away at the resources available for foreign coverage. The British international news organization even warned that cuts to its World Service would reduce it to a second-rate operation seceding its global dominance to Russia's controversial Russia Today network and Chinese state-run broadcasters.[5] As shrinking news budgets force bureaus to close, more news organizations are relying on freelancers and new ways of newsgathering to fill the foreign news hole.

The fewer number of full-time journalists dedicated to the coverage of foreign news doesn't mean there are fewer stories to tell. Instead, news from all corners of the world has demanded our attention and forced its way into our daily conversations around workplace water coolers. There are just fewer of the traditional kind of foreign correspondents who are telling them, and more freelancers filling that void.

The impact of the Islamic State in the Middle East and around the world, Russia's new Cold War-like relationship with the West, China's continued emergence as a global power, the instability of the eurozone, far-flung disasters, Cuba, migrant worker deaths at Qatar's 2022 FIFA World Cup construction sites, and even the possible future of a fractured United Kingdom are all stories that affect news consumers around the world and dominate global news.

Without two simultaneous wars consuming the bulk of the foreign news hole for the last decade, more time and resources are being spent elsewhere to report on the stories we've been missing for many years: including the plight of the persecuted Rohingya Muslim minority in Myanmar, climate change, and decades of corruption in soccer's multi-billion-dollar international governing body, FIFA.

On many occasions, even as budgets for foreign newsgathering shrink, it's been foreign news helping news organizations by cashing in on audiences captivated by big international stories. When Malaysia Airlines Flight 370 disappeared while flying from Kuala Lumpur to Beijing in 2013, CNN's ratings soared, "rising by almost 100 percent in prime time" and winning key advertising demos.[6] Also in 2013, the globe-spanning Edward Snowden NSA leak saga thrust Britain's *Guardian* newspaper and its American digital presence into an international spotlight earning the outlet awards for its coverage.[7]

But new players in international news are also creating new opportunities and new channels for stories. GlobalPost, an online news organization founded in 2009 by former *Boston Globe* foreign correspondent Charles M. Sennott, aims to transform international news coverage. GlobalPost lists correspondents in international hubs such as the UK and Japan, as well as remote locations like Senegal and Vietnam. The news site also relies on freelancers to help fill holes in newsgathering and content and also reached a deal with NBC News in 2013 to share its correspondents, reports, and video with the broadcaster.

Meanwhile, BuzzFeed, the *Huffington Post*, and *Business Insider* have all expanded their reach with international editions in places including India and Australia, as well as new efforts to recruit journalists to generate content overseas. VICE News has also invested in foreign video documentaries and newsgathering. Its partnership with HBO has also brought it to the frontlines of U.S. drone strikes in Pakistan, highlighted discrimination against gays in Uganda, and drew attention to looters in Egypt cashing in on ancient history. But its greatest achievement might be luring in the young millennial audience advertisers covet—while generating interest and investments from traditional media conglomerates such as Rupert Murdoch's 21st Century Fox.

The process of foreign newsgathering has also fundamentally changed—especially in legacy mainstream media. Journalists used to file regular dispatches from their fully staffed bureaus in cities like Nairobi and Buenos Aires. Now, international newsgathering has been centralized in hubs like London or Beijing. These bureaus—or in some cases, slim shell operations—are responsible for covering large swaths of the world, even entire continents.

Not only that, but the idea and definition of a "bureau" is changing. These days it might not necessarily be a brick-and-mortar building with a budget that includes translators and drivers, but a correspondent with a laptop and some additional equipment working out of his apartment. In some cases, there might be no "bureau" presence in an area whatsoever. Instead, a reporter based in Phoenix or Miami might be in charge of the "Latin America Bureau, flying to stories there as needed."

Much of the current international news coverage has also been transformed into crisis reporting. Audiences are saturated with news from major international crises and disasters—from massive deadly plane crashes and flare-ups in Middle East tensions, to disease outbreaks and earthquakes. This plays into "parachute journalism" and the media's "restless searchlight" that Harvard University John F. Kennedy School of Government's Pippa Norris described back in 1995.[8]

The seasoned aging correspondents, who understood the complexities of their overseas beats, now parachute into news events across the globe like pilots staying for a layover. Then, the media's impatient searchlight shines its slim focused beam on another tragedy on the other side of the world, ignoring the lingering consequences of its last interest.

This is clearly not ideal. It means news organizations focus narrowly on what's immediately playing out in one region of the world only. And, at the same time, they ignore other equally or more important news that happens elsewhere while dispatching their parachute correspondents who arrive with little local insight, sling shot from one country to another. That forces news coverage to lose valuable and important context and depth that audiences deserve.

However, from these seismic shifts in how international news is reported, freelance journalists are finding themselves more essential to the modern newsgathering process. Facing a shortage of full-time foreign correspondents, news organizations are now relying more on freelance journalists, often called "stringers."[9]

In many cases, these freelancers weave together a living through "strings" or clients: news organizations that pay freelancers for their work. Freelancers could work for these strings as infrequently as once a year, or as frequently as every day. Their relationships could've been born out of their clients' immediate need of coverage during a time of breaking news or coddled through years of casual work and trust building.

And while it's difficult to fully estimate the growth of the number of freelance foreign correspondents around the world, it's safe to estimate it is hundreds, if not thousands of journalists. The Frontline Freelance Register, an advocacy group of freelancers "who take physical risks in their work," lists the number of its members in its database at about 540 at the time of this book's publication. This shows that freelancing has become a viable career option for many—including *you.*

But, of course, not every freelance journalist abroad works in dangerous locations. Some report on financial, regulatory, business or trade news like the minutiae of developing restrictions in mining and oil exploration, and the status of lawsuits against multinationals from the safety and security of international cities such as Amsterdam and Geneva. Other journalists focus on politics like the dynamics of European Union governance in Brussels. Some reporters solely write travel and feature stories, filing dispatches from new hotels or cruise ships. Hell, even writing for a personal blog in a foreign country might qualify someone to call himself a "freelance foreign correspondent." The medium doesn't matter.

Essentially, there is no prerequisite to be a foreign correspondent. There is no international standard, universally recognized accrediting body, or even educational requirements. Anyone can be a freelance foreign correspondent.

Recognizing that, however, means a prospective freelance foreign correspondent should have experience in journalism as an editor, reporter, producer, or similar role. Ideally, they might also need a university education and contacts at news organizations willing to accept their work. A background studying the language, politics, and history of their target country is also beneficial. But the only skill required is the ability to tell accurate, factual stories through words, photos, or digital media.

This democracy in the free market of freelance foreign correspondents allows journalists of every age and level of experience to enter the world of foreign correspondence—a reporting opportunity traditionally given to privileged reporters who were groomed by news organizations as they rose through the ranks either in the bureau system in a support role or at home working on a domestic beat.

In a 1992 survey published in the book *International News and Foreign Correspondents,* Stephen Hess found many revealing facts about who these "foreign correspondents" at the time were—just before the internet started to revolutionize newsgathering and storytelling. Hess found almost 92 percent of the foreign correspondents he surveyed were white.[10] At least 61 percent were male.[11] The majority of the correspondents he surveyed also went to "highly selective" private universities.[12]

Most of the foreign correspondents Hess surveyed were likely a product of the model of the old newspaper and broadcast system. They had a pedigree education, came from a famous family, or had deep connections with leaders throughout the media industry. They traveled with expense accounts, slept in fine hotels, and had a network of support staff.

But industry progress, diversity programs, evolving hiring practices, and emerging digital opportunities have forced times to change. They've burst open the doors to people of every background to enjoy a career in international newsgathering. Today, most foreign correspondents—at least most freelancers—don't stay at the Mandarin Oriental while in Bangkok covering a coup. Instead, they cobble together a life of work based on relationships, talent, and business skills from wherever they are in the world. But paltry sporadic pay and long work hours haven't prevented floods of journalists looking for reporting opportunities overseas. If anything, these seismic shifts have shaken the industry allowing for the entrance of any journalist eager to make her mark on international news.

Today, for an ambitious, enterprising and globally curious journalist tired of the endless cycle of local school board meetings, car wrecks, and budget stories, freelancing as a foreign correspondent allows you to write home and tell the world's *other* stories.

Notes

1 Enda, Jodi. "Retreating from the World," *American Journalism Review*, December/January 2011, http://ajrarchive.org/Article.asp?id=4985.

2 Mullin, Benjamin. "McClatchy to Shutter Foreign Bureaus in Reorganization of D.C. Operation," Poynter, October 12, 2015, http://www.poynter.org/news/mediawire/378166/mcclatchy-to-shutter-foreign-bureaus-in-reorganization-of-d-c-operation/. Accessed October 12, 2015.

3 Constable, Pamela. "Demise of the Foreign Correspondent," *Washington Post*, February 18, 2007, http://www.washingtonpost.com/wp-dyn/content/article/2007/02/16/AR2007021601713.html.

4 Tyndall, Andrew, cited in Jurkowitz, Mark. "What the Digital News Boom means for Consumers," Pew Research Center's *State of the Media*, March 26, 2014, http://www.journalism.org/2014/03/26/what-the-digital-news-boom-means-for-consumers/.

5 Plunkett, John. "World Service Cuts will reduce UK's Global 'Soft Power', BBC report warns," *Guardian*, January 28, 2015, http://tinyurl.com/pxgyt8f.

6 Carter, Bill. "CNN's Ratings Surge Covering the Mystery of the Missing Airliner," *New York Times*, March 17, 2014, http://tinyurl.com/oc78j4k.

7 Wolff, Michael. "Wolff: Snowden Effect hits 'Guardian,'" *USA TODAY*, March 20, 2015, http://tinyurl.com/ncegxd8.

8 Norris, Pippa. "The Restless Searchlight: Network News Framing of the Post-Cold War World," *Political Communications* 12 no. 4 (1995), http://www.hks.harvard.edu/fs/pnorris/Acrobat/Restless%20Searchlight.pdf.

9 Bender, Bryan. "Perils Abound for Freelance Reporters in Hot Spots," *Boston Globe*, August 28, 2014, http://tinyurl.com/nlha5rn.

10 Hess, Stephen. *International News & Foreign Correspondents* (Washington, D.C.: The Brookings Institution, 1996), 154.

11 Hess, 154.

12 Hess, 154.

ACKNOWLEDGEMENTS

The Global Freelancer: Telling & Selling Foreign News wouldn't have been possible without the insight and experiences of dozens of journalists, educators, and press advocates around the world including: Andy Beale, freelance journalist; Armin Rosen, defense and military editor, *Business Insider*; Balint Szlanko, freelance foreign correspondent, Frontline Freelance Register; Bill Gentile, professor at the American University; Bob Tinsley, Proposal Development Director, International Center for Journalists; Bradley Secker, freelance photojournalist; Bridgette Auger, freelance foreign correspondent; Carey Wagner, freelance photojournalist; Cengiz Yar, freelance photojournalist; Chris Cramer, Global Head of Video, *Wall Street Journal*; Colin Cosier, freelance foreign correspondent; Daniel Bach, producer, CBC; David Rohde, investigative reporter, Reuters; Elisabet Cantenys, Head of Programmes, Rory Peck Trust; Fons Tunistra, former foreign correspondent; John Huddy, correspondent, FOX News, Jerusalem; John O'Dowd, producer, CKNW Radio; Joshua Baker, freelance journalist; Maria Korolov, former foreign correspondent; Melody Schreiber, Program Manager, International Reporting Project; Nick Barnets, freelance foreign correspondent; Nicolas Axelrod, freelance foreign correspondent; Patrick St. Michel, freelance foreign correspondent; Rob Mahoney, Deputy Executive Director, Committee to Protect Journalists; Robert Goddyn, freelance photojournalist; Robert Steiner, Director of Fellowships in Global Journalism, Munk School of Global Affairs, University of Toronto; Sam Lowenberg, freelance foreign correspondent; Steve Redisch, Executive Editor, Voice of America; Stuart Hughes, Senior World Affairs Producer, BBC; Trevor Knoblich, Digital Director, Online News Association; Zack Baddorf, freelance journalist.

Several news organizations also graciously allowed their stories to be reprinted in this book as examples of fine foreign correspondence:

"Saudi Overhaul reshapes Islam's Holiest City Mecca," Aya Batrawy for the Associated Press
"This is how ISIS smuggles Oil," Mike Giglio for BuzzFeed
"Myanmar's Mine Raiders," Patrick Winn for GlobalPost
"London's Poppies prove the Value of Public Art," Stephen Beard for American Public Media's *Marketplace*

INTRODUCTION

I wrote in black permanent marker: "PRESS" on the front and back of a light blue multi-pocket vest I had just bought outside a mosque only a couple blocks from my apartment in Tepebaşı, Istanbul.

The khaki version was sold out so I didn't quite look like the image I had in my mind of a brave, confident Peter Jennings reporting from a conflict zone with tan cargo pants and a matching sagging vest, to hold all the things foreign correspondents . . . hold.

Instead, I looked like a blue bootlegged "foreign correspondent" wannabe, with just a reporter's notebook and my iPod Touch as my only means to cover the rioting that had taken over Istanbul's touristy Taksim Square. I had no high-priced DSLR, professional audio recording equipment, or even any experience reporting outside the United States. I barely spoke Turkish. All I had was the ability to sniff out news and write.

Regardless, I thought: "It's official. I'm a foreign correspondent."

I was determined to make this my entrée into a career as a freelance foreign correspondent.

I had already been in Istanbul for two months struggling to gather enough "strings" (freelance clients) after I arrived on a one-way ticket from Washington, D.C.'s Dulles Airport alone, not knowing a soul. Istanbul was as familiar of a place to me as Mars was.

Not only that, but starting a one-man business operation here was quickly driving me bankrupt. The expenses of moving to a new country, and getting started as a freelance foreign correspondent there were finally starting to make me question my commitment to my new career. I saw desperately needed dollar signs amid the relentless onslaught of live televised havoc across parts of Istanbul and Turkey. Plus, I had to find some way to pay for my Doner kebab addiction (they may be cheap, but they really add up in both money and inches).

Not only didn't I have the right outfit, equipment, or budget, but I had no body armor, gas mask, helmet, or really anything to offer me any protection whatsoever from the hurling rocks, rubber bullets, and tear gas that suffocated protesters. I looked out of place, since full-time foreign correspondents from outlets like CNN had protective vests and helmets.

But I ventured into the chaos outside my doorstep without thinking twice. It's the type of fearless foolishness that only youth and reporters have: in my case, a dangerous combination.

Protesters—demanding more freedoms from Turkey's authoritarian Prime Minister Tayyip Erdoğan—destroyed ATMs, smashed storefront windows, set the carcasses of public buses and police vehicles on fire and even overturned television news live trucks.

Graffiti like "Tayyip is my girl" were scrawled over signs and storefronts in the trendy, expensive Istiklal Street—a main artery in European Istanbul and center for designer clothing stores and upscale boutiques. The stores that weren't destroyed were shuttered with metal gates or had their windows boarded up as if waiting for a hurricane to pass.

This went on for days. The unrest was so transformative police gave up. They fled Taksim Square and protesters took over—but a sort of peace fell over the area instead of lawlessness.

Young Turks lit red paper Chinese lanterns in the evenings as if celebrating a chance to breathe and sending prayers for peace to Heaven. Old Turks who couldn't brave the crowds and summer heat of the protests leaned out of their windows onto the street in the evenings banging pots and pans in support of demonstrators as a citywide chorus of clanking was heard.

Entrepreneurial Istanbulites sold bottles of water, hot tea, watermelon, sandwiches, and even unregulated alcohol to the thousands of young protesters and international media who gathered to watch tired Turks take a stand against their government.

Protesters rallied in Gezi Park—the small sanctuary of green in a growing pit of concrete and steel. The government's plans to demolish it and build yet another mall sparked the massive protests after a small group of protesters trying to protect the park from construction crews were pepper sprayed by police. An image of a woman in a red dress being sprayed by an officer symbolized the oppression of people only exercising their right to be heard. The photo spread like wildfire through social media and international news organizations.

But the protests grew from more than just an environmental movement in a sprawling ancient city entering a new modern renaissance with its eyes on hosting the 2020 summer Olympics. The demonstrations represented a thorn in the side of Turkey's ruling government officials who often did what they wanted, regardless of the effects or consequences to the people of this democratic secular republic that was increasingly anything but.

For years, authorities had arrested journalists, bulldozed history to make way for shopping centers, and threatened dissidents. In the wake of Tahrir Square in Cairo, and the Arab Spring that swept through the rest of North Africa and the Middle East, many Turks felt that this was their chance for change.

I felt like I was standing at the front door of history. I was watching a nation demand a new future and a new government. I could feel the sense of hope in Gezi Park. It was everywhere. The sounds of beating drum circles, the lingering sting of tear gas confronting the smoky ashes of burned-out police vehicles, and the blocks of sharp political graffiti signaled something big was coming.

But the government wasn't going to back down without a fight.

Soon—the party was cut short. Police in armored tanks, and on the ground carrying weapons loaded with rubber bullets and tear gas, moved in and cleared out everyone but the few angry protesters who lit small fires and confronted tired and weary officers.

And there I was: stepping over rubble, broken glass, and piles of garbage in my cheap, blue "foreign correspondent's vest" trying to make a name for myself in Istanbul and back at home.

After spending years as a local TV reporter covering shootings, car crashes, and murders, I got tired of knocking on the doors of dead relatives to shove a mic in someone's face. I didn't feel like my work had an impact. I wasn't excited to be a journalist anymore.

Occasionally, a long investigative report or a thrilling week covering a battering hurricane would perk me up. But the endless and pointless daily grind of general assignment reporting began to take its toll. I knew I couldn't stay in local news for the next 30 years of my career: I had to make a change.

So I quit my job. I bought a one-way ticket to Istanbul with no experience as a freelancer or with foreign news. But I never looked back.

My saving grace was my fragile new string with CBS Radio News in New York I had spun before I left the U.S. While visiting Manhattan months before I arrived in Turkey, CBS agreed to take a chance on me and accept my pitches from Istanbul. Although there was no guarantee of paid opportunities, I felt lucky to have a lead on casual work. I had no background in radio, and certainly not enough to work for the same radio news organization Edward R. Murrow helped build as a foreign correspondent based in Europe during World War II contributing to the same morning newscast I was, the "CBS World News Roundup."

Finally, those visits to New York staying on a friend's couch, and the weeks of cold calling and brief foot-in-the-door visits began to pay off, at least with CBS. I began to gather audio of chanting protesters, police firing canisters of American-made tear gas into crowds and young men returning fire with Molotov cocktails. Every hour or so I sent reports to CBS as the protests and clashes with police heated up. Radio stations from the U.S. and Canada were all calling me asking for live reports.

At one point—feeling invincible because I was a "journalist," I ventured closer to the heart of the action. There, I found myself isolated. Through a thick, piercing cloud of suffocating tear gas I saw menacing white armored police vehicles creeping toward me. Officers stood behind them clearly aiming tear gas canisters guns at me, along with flash-bang grenades, as the large vehicles aimed their notorious water jets at me. I was more worried about my cell phone and iPod getting ruined from the water than my own safety. Clearly my "PRESS" vest was useless.

So I backed up and took a more cautious approach to my coverage. I was able to track down CBS's Holly Williams, a correspondent for television who lived in Istanbul, and her crew, including a producer from the London bureau. They were gracious enough to give me a gas mask, goggles, and helmet—although I think they were meant more for construction workers than conflict reporters. I was grateful nonetheless.

For several weeks I covered the protests that lingered in Istanbul's government and economic center. I also recruited new strings, including FOX News, Voice of America, CBC, and many others. I began to cover other stories such as the worsening civil war in Syria and the flood of refugees who were seeking new lives in Turkey. I turned down opportunities to report from Aleppo in Syria, instead focusing on the opposition headquarters based in Istanbul—a wise decision. Many brave journalists have risked their lives covering Syria, often being kidnapped and killed by militants.

I eventually left Istanbul several months later to cover other parts of the world as news slowed down and Istanbul lost its bid to host the 2020 Olympics. The Turkish tiger began to stumble—its emerging powerhouse economy mired in petty regulations and uncertainty. Its fountain of stories that had so intrigued newsrooms across the world began to dry up.

But the effects of those summer 2013 protests still have an effect on Turkish politics and national sentiments. For all that it accomplished in disrupting and antagonizing the government—it only strengthened Erdoğan. He cast the unrest and new opponents to his regime as enemies of Islam. He labeled the international media—especially CNN—and, even multinational banks, as foreign instigators colluding to push up interest rates to ruin the country's economy and bring Turkey down. Erdoğan doubled down on inflammatory rhetoric and callousness until his Justice and Development Party finally lost its ruling majority stranglehold in a decisive election in June 2015.

The anti-government protests frankly showed the world how whacky Turkey's government was. It jeopardized its half-hearted bid to enter the European Union, and it only put more distance between Turkey and the U.S., who had been strong public allies before the unrest.

But it also baptized me into the religion of foreign news reporting. I was addicted. I felt like for once in my career—however short thus far—my work had meaning. I wrote home with stories that had value. They weren't poodle parades or days'-long snowstorms or actual cats stuck in trees. They were transformative, historical events that I was witnessing first hand.

You, too, have the opportunity to tell the world's stories. It doesn't take years riding the city beat, logging countless hours of tape late into the evening for a grouchy producer on the foreign desk, or dreaming about witnessing the world's future from your home computer while watching as your Facebook newsfeed shows the adventures of your globetrotting friends as you pick stray Cheetos off your sweatpants.

Use this book as a guide to map out your personal journey to Nairobi or New Delhi. You don't have to be an award-winning journalist, or a child of a Vanderbilt, to see the world and pay the bills as a freelance foreign correspondent. You won't get rich, but you'll deposit stories into your portfolio, memory, diary, and even social media accounts that people around the world only see on TV, where you're seeing them in person. All it takes is dedication, careful planning, and a bit of enterprising business-savvy legwork.

Good luck.

PART I

Getting Started

1

PREPARING YOURSELF

The opportunities and experiences working as a freelance foreign correspondent provides are limitless—but so are the risks and potential pitfalls.

Uprooting your life and traveling across the world without the guarantee of a steady paycheck is not something to take lightly. It can end relationships, plunge you into debt, and even *stall* your career. But, if you're successful, the move could re-energize your love of journalism, allow you to make the world your office, introduce you to characters and people who could transform your global outlook, and push your limits.

So before you go, consider asking yourself *why*, before *how*. Are you escaping a limited career path at a local paper in Paducah? Are you running away from a ruined relationship? What do you want to accomplish? Are there no other trails for you to blaze at home or where you currently are? Do you think you're ready? What do you have to lose by staying and what do you have to gain by going?

Deciding to Go

For many journalists who've boarded a flight on a one-way ticket to a foreign destination to begin a new life, deciding to work as a freelance foreign correspondent came after months, if not years, of dissatisfaction with their career or even their own lives.

In the 1990s, young Chicago journalist Maria Korolov dreamed of working as a foreign correspondent—especially for her then-employer the *Chicago Tribune*.

Only a year out of college, Korolov approached the newspaper's editor asking how she could report overseas.

"He said, 'First you work in a suburb' [for the newspaper] which is what I was doing, 'then, you work your way up to the city [desk], then you work at the state level, then you work at the national level, then you go overseas,'" she says. "And I'm like 'I'll be 50 by then!'"

"And he was like, 'Yeah. That's how old our foreign correspondents are.'"

But that wouldn't satisfy Korolov.

"I was like, 'What's the other way to do it?'"

"He said, 'Well you know, I can't recommend this personally, but I hear that young people just go over there and they just try to find work. But if you do decide to do this option don't expect our bureau to take you in. There's no guarantee. This is a very risky thing.'"

So she thought to herself, "This is the way to get started."

Korolov skipped her last month's rent and used it to buy a plane ticket overseas.

She only had two requirements for a target country: it had to have a language she spoke and a couch on which to crash.

Fortunately for Korolov, she had a grandmother in Moscow and she spoke broken Russian she remembered from her childhood. She was born in Leningrad before she emigrated to the U.S. as a young child with her parents in the late 1970s.

Her Russian was barely usable at first when she returned to the country decades later, but she made it work and took advantage of her connections there.

Ultimately, it wasn't a hard decision for Korolov who lusted for something more than what the Chicago suburbs could offer her.

Korolov says, "There are people who say 'I'm hoping it comes along, but I've got other stuff.'"

Korolov didn't want to take a chance and spend years riding the well-worn path to a foreign bureau. Instead, she wanted to do it immediately. She wanted to be in control of her own future.

"Once I decided I was going to go overseas the question became how, instead of will anyone ever send me?" she says.

Another freelance foreign correspondent, Nick Barnets, took a similar path, but leading instead to Greece.

Even while working for CBS News as a 2012 election researcher and a photographer for television station NY1, Barnets wanted something more.

"When I started out in news, I always wanted to do international news because I grew up in two different countries that being the U.S. and Greece," Barnets says. "I developed a sense of the importance of international news, and why it's important for Americans especially to know what's going on around the world."

But, like Korolov, Barnets was frustrated with the pace of his career toward his goals.

"I decided I couldn't go much farther while staying in New York to fulfill my goals of being an international journalist," he says.

So Barnets targeted Athens, a place with which he was already familiar and whose language he spoke. He now counts CBS Radio News as one of his strings.

Carey Wagner, a freelance photojournalist and cinematographer now based in Brooklyn, wanted to pursue more stories that made "a contribution to society."

Although Wagner was satisfied with her work as a staff photographer at the *Sun-Sentinel* in South Florida she wanted to do lengthier examinations of communities across the world.

"I'm interested in thinking globally," Wagner says.

She knew there were many communities, particularly Latinos in South Florida, that were impacted by news in other parts of the world like Latin America.

"It's important to realize where we come from, and the connections we have around the world," she says.

She was especially interested in focusing her work on human rights and women's issues.

"Not everyone is living and expressing themselves in a way that I would say is completely free," Wagner says. "It's great to be able to connect with other women. I find it empowering."

But Wagner's decision to pursue her professional interests independently wasn't easy.

"When I finally decided to leave, which was a very hard decision, I wanted to dedicate as much time as I could to telling stories I thought were important," she remembers.

Wagner has since targeted her reporting on many stories abroad including child grooms in Nepal, sex workers in India, and religious communities in Indonesia.

For Daniel Bach, who now lives and works as a host and producer for CBC in Toronto, he piggybacked on the opportunity to freelance overseas through his girlfriend.

"I have a lot of experience in travel and so there was an opportunity with my partner to go live in France for a while," Bach says.

It was an opportunity to follow his own interests while continuing a relationship.

"International news has always been my interest area, even way back in high school," Bach recalls. "I always wanted to be involved in covering [international] news in some form."

Bach worked primarily freelancing as a radio journalist not only in France, but also in the UK, and the Czech Republic. He says a journalism course he took in Prague helped initially prepare him for working as a freelance foreign correspondent: "Much of the toolkit and network I had as a foreign journalist came from the course."

But Bach also relied on his network of contacts at CBC in Canada, where he had also worked prior to his experience in France: "It would have been much more difficult for me to sell stories at the start as well, had I not had a working relationship with CBC assignment producers from my time in Toronto," he says.

In the world of freelance foreign correspondents, the stories of Korolov, Barnets, Wagner, and Bach are similar. Many others have followed the same goals, if not different paths.

And today, perhaps more than ever, as the way newsgathering changes, the chance to follow similar career paths is becoming an even clearer choice for many journalists toiling away covering school board meetings for a shrinking news organization that offers fewer and fewer opportunities for them year after year. Your time to prepare starts now. No matter where you are in your career, time could be your biggest advantage.

A Changing Industry, and Changing Career

Stuart Hughes, diplomatic producer for BBC News, has played a role in the massive global news organization's foreign newsgathering efforts for decades. He's watched the broadcaster and its industry evolve.

"The industry is becoming more reliant on freelancers," Hughes says. "Few organizations can afford a network of bureaus. So the work falls to freelancers."

Traditional brick-and-mortar bureaus have many expenses: staff correspondents, costly equipment sometimes including satellite trucks and professional video cameras, translators, drivers, and even a finance department to track expenses.

"You're doing business in another country," says Steve Redisch, Voice of America executive editor and former CNN deputy Washington bureau chief.

Having a physical presence in another country often means news organizations must follow foreign regulations and ensure overseas tax compliance while coordinating with government authorities in the target country and negotiating hiring and personnel practices.

"As an executive, you have to make a decision of whether that cost—that investment—is worth what you are going to get out of there," Redisch says.

The U.S. government-funded VOA has hub bureaus in London and Johannesburg, and smaller operations in Moscow, Islamabad, and elsewhere. But through the years, the massive news organization that targets its broadcasts and digital efforts to audiences overseas has scaled back. It has closed bureaus and shifted resources as news priorities and newsgathering methods have changed.

"For a lot of years, the reason why organizations had a lot of bureaus was for communications," he says.

Twenty-five years ago, television crews in remote areas of the Middle East, such as those covering the Gulf War, depended on fixed locations at which they could feed video back home and do live shots. That often meant returning to a bureau in Baghdad or Kuwait and using a large satellite dish to feed content back—infrastructure that couldn't easily be moved.

In some cases, television networks used a costly mobile satellite system. Correspondents such as NBC's David Bloom and his cameraman Craig White could send video footage back during the 2003 invasion of Iraq through one of these systems. The Battlefield Satellite Newsgathering System, dubbed "the Bloommobile System" after the reporter's early death from pulmonary embolism, included a gyro-stablized camera in an armored U.S. Army vehicle, and transmission equipment mounted in a protective dome in a trailing truck.[1] The network deployed the system again in 2010 to transmit live video of a convoy with U.S. combat troops leaving Iraq.[2]

Since then, smaller, cheaper, and more easily transportable digital newsgathering equipment has displaced expensive satellite systems at fixed locations using cumbersome infrastructure and costly satellite time. FTP has allowed broadcast news crews to transmit video anywhere with decent Wi-Fi or mobile broadband connectivity. Even once high-tech Broadband Global Area Network (BGAN) units—which were essential to covering stories in poorly-connected locations like war zones—are now mostly obsolete. Basically satellite phones, the units provided marginal live shot and data connectivity with usually slow uploading times. But some crews in conflict zones worry they act as target beacons to forces such as Syria's Bashar al-Assad who can allegedly locate the transmission point to launch an attack.

The developments in technology have also changed field crew assignments and responsibilities. No longer are four-person crews necessary to cover a story abroad. Although they still exist today, especially in unionized domestic newsgathering in the U.S.—employing a video photographer, producer, sound engineer, and correspondent is costly. News organizations aren't just paying for their time on assignment, but also their daily expenses like hotels, food, incidentals, and insurance.

These days it's likely you'll find that traditional crew family split in half.

Major broadcasters like VOA and ABC News rely on reporters who can do it all: shoot, write, edit, and feed back a live shot if needed. Sometimes the roles are divided between two people, for example, a reporter who produces and writes a story, and a photographer who shoots and edits it—a team you'll often find in many larger local television markets in the U.S.

Some digital journalists are even shooting video entirely on smartphones, like some who work at Al Jazeera's digital outlet AJ+. It's a model that might just catch on.

"I also think about using digital assets first," Redisch says.

This method of "backpack journalism" is not logistically possible in all cases—even many of its hardcore advocates admit that. For instance, if a network interviews a head of state, being able to professionally light the person and shoot it—sometimes with multiple cameras—is too time consuming a task for a solo journalist and an important official with only minutes to spare for an interview. It can also be too dangerous for a solo digital journalist to operate effectively in a conflict zone, where having a partner to watch your back can literally be the difference between life and death.

Sometimes, in foreign locations with only occasional news that would be of interest to international audiences, say perhaps in Bangalore, a "fixer" will do all these tasks. A fixer does many things—and can really live up to his nickname in the trade: he can fix things. Fixers—often locals or longtime foreign journalists based in-country hired by a large news organization to assist an out-of-town crew—can make miracles happen. They often arrange access to authorities and officials for interviews, help coordinate technical logistics for a shoot, and sometimes even drive or translate. They have intimate knowledge of a location and often come recommended by other journalists.

Digital newsgathering has also transformed crew locations and editorial priorities. News organizations now often rely on single-person "bureaus" staffed with these new digital journalists instead of full-fledged, fully staffed bureaus.

"It's all portable, it's all mobile," Redisch says. "You don't have a place to go. You can do it all on your own now."

News organizations are also dedicating resources once meant for foreign coverage, to other priorities like developing content for Facebook and YouTube. This is also helping make an expensive, accomplished, seasoned old-media foreign correspondent a relic of news history. In many cases, except for positions meant for rising stars like chief European correspondents, these veterans are being replaced with much cheaper stringers. Many of these stringers are young, and can easily navigate the demands and developments of modern-day newsroom editorial priorities like Snapchat and Twitter.

In larger hub bureaus, stringers might also help supplement the coverage of full-time foreign correspondents, as is the case at VOA, according to Redisch. The American broadcaster relies on stringers to cover "day-to-day" news, which frees up staff reporters to cover "thematic" stories with sweeping time-consuming work and context.

The Payoff (Or Not)

These changes in how news is covered abroad and who covers it have tempted many journalists who see new opportunities for them. But Hughes warns as the number of freelancers working abroad increases, so does the competition.

"Don't expect an easy way to make a living," he says.

For many, however, the risks have paid off—if not financially, then professionally or personally.

"I think it has certainly benefitted my career," Barnets says.

While working in New York, Barnets says he was often a faceless content generator. Now his name is attached to real reporting.

"Before I came here none of my work had my own signature on it," he says. "I didn't do anything that had my own name on it."

Barnets also gets to do what he enjoys the most: traveling and cultural exploration. During his time in Athens, he has visited Moscow, Istanbul, London, and Cyprus.

Bach finds his overseas experience helpful to reporting on foreign current events back at home in Canada.

"I always found that it has given me a different insight into how stories can be covered," Bach says.

From Toronto, Bach covered the aftermath of the deadly January 2015 attacks on the French satirical newspaper *Charlie Hebdo* in Paris.

"Knowing how emergency services communicate [in France], and how information generally comes out from the French government," he says, "I could anticipate how things would play out."

In my case: freelancing as a foreign correspondent benefited me in two ways. It allowed me to cover the kind of history making international news I'd always craved, and earned me valuable, hard-to-get professional credibility back home. My work overseas opened doors at large news organizations such as FOX and CBS that would have never been possible had I stuck with covering car wrecks and robberies while working in local TV. It also earned me street clout as a reporter with a reputation for covering challenging big news from around the world in any environment. Through my work overseas, I demonstrated storytelling in every medium: radio, television, online, and in print. These skills and experiences are essential to journalists replacing the "dinosaurs" of old media.

Many people set out abroad determined to report and be the next Christiane Amanpour. Many fail—they come home without a single clip in their portfolio, mountains of debt, and a sore ego. But, recognize the potential and new opportunities with which reporting at a foreign destination offers, and then weigh what you're willing to risk and sacrifice to make it pay off. Although it feels like you're alone on this path, many others have helped clear the way. Rely on their wisdom and their lessons from failure.

Stripping Down, Saving Up

Like Ryan Bingham in *Up in the Air* (played by George Clooney in the 2009 movie), a global free-lancer's life must be carry-on sized.

Just about everything I own fits into my blue REI 40-liter "Lookout" backpack. My clothes, my toothbrush, my laptop, and iPhone all fit into the crushing tiny space between some stranger's case of fish sauce and a baby's stroller in the overhead compartment. And soon, even that backpack might be too large—as airlines shrink how much they allow passengers to stash in crowded overhead bins as checked baggage fees rise.

Regardless, downsizing your life ensures mobility and freedom. Maybe Buddhists are right after all.

Slimming down your life—and all your possessions—means you can easily move to where the news is happening. For instance, if you first arrive in Tbilisi, Georgia, but a flare-up along the country's border with Russia promises to offer weeks worth of work, it might be wise to relocate to an area closer to locations in which you can more easily gather news, interview militants, and attend last-minute press conferences. Not having to transport all your belongings and valuable equipment in a cross-country caravan—but rather easily hop on a cheap domestic flight—leaves you in a better position to commit to where the news is without having to maintain a separate home or place for your accumulating belongings elsewhere on a freelancer's budget.

I believe that this is the new kind of "backpack journalism." It's not just a method of carrying only must-have digital newsgathering equipment, but living with only your essential possessions and even personal obligations.

But, of course, this mobile lifestyle is dependent on not just whether there is enough self-sustaining news, but if you've secured strings and are successful in finding new living arrangements or at least temporary accommodations that won't drain your income. You'll also need to slim down your attachments to home to strip down to the basics in your life.

When I left my exhausting television reporting job in Raleigh-Durham, North Carolina, I took things a step farther. I sold my car, moved out of my $1,200 per month downtown apartment, sold all my furniture to strangers on Craigslist, and reclaimed my childhood bedroom at my parents' house in an isolated leafy suburb of Baltimore.

I wasn't living the life all millennials dream about years after they graduate college. But I was doing it to make my dream a reality. I didn't care about having to pick up dates in my mom's car or avoiding high school classmates at the local Walmart for a few months while I saved up enough cash to launch my career. I was prepared to do it. My only focus was chasing my dream.

Got pets? You might as well leave them behind, because the red tape of far-flung countries and even the quarantine procedures of first-world nations aren't going to be very kind to them.

Relationships? You better learn how to date long distance, if your mate won't come along for the ride and you can't break things off.

Even family obligations can sidetrack the career aspirations of freelance foreign correspondents. Your parents might be sick. Or, maybe a relative has suddenly become unemployed and is now dependent on the help of their family. Whatever the case: never neglect your family or moral responsibilities. Now might not be the time to make the transition abroad, but that doesn't mean it won't ever be. Wait for your situation to mature, use the time to do early preparations for your trip, and remain focused on your goals.

No matter your situation, sacrificing the attachments you're able to eliminate with your home life with few consequences will make life overseas less distracting. It will also pale in comparison to the sacrifices you'll make once you actually get there: like finding a home with working plumbing. If you're going pretty much anywhere east of Greece, look forward to shitting in a porcelain hole and "wiping" with a hose.

By doing this: I eliminated the burdens of paying a monthly car loan, rent, a costly gym membership, and even a Netflix subscription. It liberated me while I saved up at home, and also as I began my journey overseas. It allowed me to fully concentrate on a new career without having to worry about subletting my apartment or who was going to water my peace lily.

Fons Tunistra, a former freelance foreign correspondent based in China in the 1990s, recommends all journalists with plans to work independently abroad zero in on preparing financially.

"You should have your financial basics in order," Tunistra says. "If you don't have that then you have a problem."

When Tunistra began reporting in the booming city of Shanghai, he experienced the same challenges many other independent journalists working in fast-growing cities share.

"You saw the income from journalism dropping very fast, on the other hand, the cost of living was going up," he says.

Today, living expenses in Shanghai have soared.

In 2015, the global consulting firm Mercer listed Shanghai as the world's sixth most expensive city for expats to live and work in.[3]

Living and working in a city like Shanghai can be a real distraction to a freelance foreign correspondent who wants to focus on journalism but also needs to survive.

A far cry from the budget of a typical freelancer, Tunistra's full-time colleagues in large news bureaus had envious salaries and expense accounts.

"I was very jealous of all the people who had all their expenses paid, housing paid, all these things," he says.

To prepare for such financial challenges, especially if your work is in a major metropolis, Tunistra recommends you save enough money to support yourself for a year.

Barnets recommends taking similar financial measures before you get on the ground working (hopefully). "The financial uncertainty is difficult," Barnets says. He recommends saving up as much as possible to at least cover the start-up costs of getting settled and working for what could be months without a reliable or steady source of income.

Bach says even though he was living with his girlfriend in France, he still chose to save some money before he left home.

"I also set aside some money of my own, just so if things didn't go well professionally, I would be OK," he says.

Bach warns of the financial perils of trying to make a living as a freelance foreign correspondent.

"Right now, in the era of journalism we're in it can be hard to stay busy and to find people [editors] that are buying," he says.

In order for you to focus on working and supporting yourself as a freelance foreign correspondent you need to be mobile. You must be self-contained. You certainly don't need to sell your sweet downtown pad. But, if you don't find someone to pay your mortgage, that extra $2,300 a month is going to be a burden to your focus and your budget.

Remember, this is not a vacation. You won't be able to afford a freelance foreign correspondent's lifestyle and career, if you're living like it's a honeymoon. Get used to drinking the local beer and taking the bus. Say goodbye to Marriotts and hello to hostels and "couch surfing."

By cutting the strings to many of your possessions and attachments, you're gaining flexibility and proving to yourself your commitment to your future as a freelance foreign correspondent. Besides, you can always buy a new car and find a new girlfriend, right? That's what Craigslist is for.

Gearing Up

Depending on what type of journalism you might want to do overseas, this is also a good time to explore the kind of equipment you'll need to purchase.

I receive no compensation from B & H Photo Video (maybe I should), but it is a great place to start looking and shopping for multimedia equipment. They have an excellent selection of professional DSLRs, video cameras, microphones, and audio recorders. They are quick with shipping, and offer affordable prices especially on their most popular products.

However, you'll need to estimate how talented you are with shooting video, and whether it's worth investing $4,000 on a digital video camera if you don't think you'll be able to sell many video reports from your region as soon as you arrive. You first priority should be your survival, financially and physically.

Also keep in mind you don't want too much gear. In addition to your laptop, bringing too many pieces of brand new photography, video, and audio gear can make you a target for thieves and even local customs officers. Remember, you have no multinational news organization whose insurance you can rely on, and whose contacts and pocketbook you can use to get equipment into and out of countries. International customs can thwart many chances to get gear and equipment to a foreign location. Beware of this, because it may mean an unpleasant welcome as soon as your arrive.

Additionally, carrying extra accessories like too many lights, batteries, tripods, audio recorders, lavalieres, SD cards, and XLR cords will also weigh you down—and could even prevent you from concentrating on your main focus: content.

Broadcasters these days would much rather have something "exclusive" than what "looks great," according to Redisch.

If you're the only one with footage of a Syrian chemical weapons attack along with interviews of victims, no one will care about whether it was shot on a P2 card or an SD card, or if you used a shotgun mic instead of an omnidirectional handheld mic. What *is* important is that the content you *did* get is of usable quality. Save the high production values and the expensive equipment that goes along with it for a time when you have proved your success overseas and are taking in the income to support all those expenses.

However, understand digital newsgathering can be a lifesaver overseas—and it's becoming essential for all freelancers. But do it in baby steps, and at a pace that works for you.

Berlin-based American freelance foreign correspondent Samuel Loewenberg warns that stretching your focus across many media can thin your newsgathering and storytelling quality.

Lowenberg says, "Trying to do too many things at once rarely produces the best work."

But he recognizes multimedia fluency's potential as a way to enhance your reporting.

"On the other hand, I've done a handful of stories where I did the words, the images, and the video—and that's a powerful package," he says.

If you do commit to working as a multimedia journalist abroad, and scaling up with more specialized, professional equipment, review what digital newsgathering tools are available for you now at your current skill level.

Regardless, no longer can freelancers expect to make a living working with just one medium. "If all you do is take photographs, then that is only one revenue stream that you've got," says Hughes. "The more skills you've got, the more opportunities you have to sell your material."

Fortunately for freelancers, digital opportunities are providing them with new ways to earn money and ways to tell stories.

"Your eyes are so much more open to new ways of storytelling, and companies," Wagner says.

Organizations like the BBC are increasingly telling stories for social media, the web, and mobile devices, in addition to traditional television and radio platforms. They also have expectations their journalists will invest the same attention to multi-platform content.

"The big change has been the digital revolution," Hughes says. A few years ago, "Our website would have been an afterthought . . . whereas now it's moving more center stage."

But that's added to the growing list of skills needed to produce such content.

If you want a list of things somebody coming into the business should be able to do, I guess it's a little bit of everything," Hughes says. "We would expect to have a degree of radio skills, the ability to shoot if possible . . . [and] some basic editing skills."

In addition to recording and editing audio for the radio, Nick Barnets takes photos to accompany web stories he's writing.

There's also another advantage of selling photos: their use in any language, especially as a way to supplement your income as a writer.

"The benefit of being a photographer is that you can work with publications in any language, the situation is different for a print or radio journalist of course," Istanbul-based freelance photojournalist Bradley Secker says.

The best bang for your buck for a versatile digital newsgathering tool may just come from an iPhone or similar smartphone. It can do everything from streaming live video, to editing audio, to taking and filing photos instantly. It's a great tool for a "generalist" working with many different media to maximize the technology that is easily and affordably available to them.

I recommend downloading several photo and video apps for smartphones like the iPhone. I like FiLMiC Pro (USD$7.99) that allows you to manually set the exposure, frame rate, and other features to improve the quality of what you're shooting. You might also want to consider purchasing cheap clip-on lenses for your iPhone: fisheye, macro, and wide lens.

"A good iPhone—an unlocked iPhone—basically is a ticket to telling stories very easily," Bach says. He often relied on his iPhone to take and file photos, connect to social media, and access email quickly.

Having your phone unlocked is beneficial. It can then be used to make local calls at much cheaper rates with a new local SIM card, rather than relying solely on your foreign number where roaming data charges and high international calling and texting rates can add up. SIM cards can be easily purchased through a mobile phone service provider at your target destination, or in advance of your trip abroad.

Alternatively, you can carry two phones: one local phone that you only use for domestic calls while abroad, and another you have with your same number from your home country that you use sparingly as a way to receive calls from clients who might not have your new local foreign number.

Some phones—even cheap ones—can operate on multiple SIM cards with multiple numbers. This can be handy instead of carrying around two or more different devices. You can simply switch between operating, calling, and texting on one SIM card for your local number and another for your foreign home number. It's something worth considering. However, at the time of this book's publication this feature is not available on iPhones.

But beware of the quirks of calling at whatever destination from which you plan to base yourself. Many countries use pre-paid phone plans extensively—so "topping up" will be a regular necessity.

Also, in some countries like Turkey, the use of voicemail isn't as common as it is in other places like the U.S. But, fortunately, in many countries receiving calls is free, even long-distance ones.

Not only that, but in many countries free Wi-Fi hotspots are common. When I lived in Istanbul, I kept a mental note of where the closest open Wi-Fi hotspot was. Usually large coffee chains, banks, and even some entire cities allow you to easily connect to the internet without having to use your mobile phone's data plan. Generally, I can almost always count on a Starbucks or McDonald's in places across the globe to offer free Wi-Fi. Of course, be careful when using public Wi-Fi while entering sensitive information such as your financial information.

Brooklyn-based freelance foreign correspondent Zack Baddorf warns that even communicating through social media can put you, your sources, and your reporting at risk.

"Governments like Pakistan, like Egypt, and like Turkey are maliciously using social media as well," he says.

Unsecure communication channels are increasingly worrying more reporters like Baddorf who tries to convince sources to contact him through encrypted, but more inconvenient, methods.

"It's something that is going to become more and more of a challenge," he says.

In terms of software that should be standard newsgathering features on your computer, I recommend a FTP program like FileZilla. It's free, downloadable, and is simple to use. It allows you to seamlessly upload any file to the in-house server of one of your clients. The program is also widely used and trusted by many news organizations. Not all news organizations use FTP, especially from freelancers in the field. Some use a similar proprietary web-based system or similar program. But in many cases using a program like FileZilla will save you time when you need to send large audio or video files to a string.

You'll also need Skype. Obviously, it provides you with no-cost calling to other Skype users. But it also allows you to call international mobile numbers and landlines at a minimal cost on a "pay-as-you-go" plan with credit that doesn't expire. It's even cheaper to get a monthly Skype subscription that ranges from a capped number of minutes to unlimited calling to more than 170 countries and regions. Using Skype is an economical way to communicate with editors back home and also enables you to reach out to contacts and sources across borders in areas that affect your reporting in your target destination. The call quality is usually better than traditional phone calls, which is more suitable to include in broadcast pieces. However, most news organizations credit Skype when they have used it to conduct interviews with sound or video included in their live or taped reports. Skype can also be used to do a live shot in a pinch for a network or digital news organization.

You might also want to download internet-based mobile apps like Luci Live Lite (USD$29.99) and Live Report Pro (free), which many radio stations and networks use to receive live broadcast-quality reporting from the field. Dejero LIVE+ is a similar app that works with television station and network infrastructure to receive broadband-quality live video.

Free downloadable programs like Audacity, or GarageBand, which comes preloaded onto Macs, are affordable ways to edit audio for radio purposes. Another free option that you can easily download and use is the open-source Audacity program.

You also might be able to get by editing video using iMovie, but the program can be cumbersome and has limited features compared to high-end competitors like Adobe Premiere Pro and Final Cut Pro. If you are a still photographer, using a program like Adobe Photoshop is pretty much essential. If you are just getting started creating multimedia content always begin with free or affordable programs that can help teach you the basics before you invest in more powerful or specialized software.

Whatever medium you choose to work in, you'll certainly need some sort of word-processing software. Many news organizations require you draw up an invoice or write your completed story in a commonly used program like Microsoft Word. It might be possible to access a low-cost Microsoft Word license through your former employer or an educational institution. Otherwise there are free programs available like OpenOffice. Consider also downloading a complementary spreadsheet program like Microsoft Excel, which can help you keep track of expenses for tax purposes, log the development of story ideas for each string, update lists of contacts and sources, and, even better, fine tune complex expense reports and invoices. Google Docs offers a free spreadsheet program available on the Cloud, along with other handy features.

One of your priorities before you depart should also be to put whatever gear and software you purchase to use.

Take the time to thoroughly learn the quirks of your gear, apps, and programs, and figure out how to use them quickly in "run-and-gun" situations. Don't just add to the weight of your backpack, but add to your skillset too.

I produced, shot, and edited television reports for the Voice of America in Istanbul, wrote online pieces that included many of my photos for CNN and FOX News, and wrote print articles on international regulatory developments for Bloomberg BNA, in addition to reporting for the radio.

Having the skills to work seamlessly in developing multimedia content helps build your portfolio as a skilled versatile journalist, and earns you a more reliable paycheck.

Writing Home

Don't forget, your most powerful moneymaking tool is your ability to write quickly, accurately, and creatively. Unless you're a photographer, with a long list of clients willing to send you steady paychecks, your bread and butter will still be writing. Being able to create digital multimedia content will just be icing on the cake.

Ensure that you're tinkering with writing in every medium.

If you are a journalist with a background primarily in magazine writing, you might be a pro at thinking of new ways to illustrate a story through prose or adding color to dull events. But, you might not be accustomed to tight deadlines working in challenging environments outside newsrooms: anywhere from a dusty field, to a crowded protest, or a boat overflowing with desperate migrants in the heat of July in the Mediterranean. Do your best to work on this. Whereas magazine writing gives you the flexibility to weave a story through 3,000 words over several months with substantial reporting, the daily dispatches of most mainstream foreign correspondents tend to be "nuts-and-bolts" news reports from 300 to 500 words. Features, of course, can run longer.

Similarly, if your background is in newspapers—an increasing rarity these days—explore new ways of telling stories. With the growing number of digital opportunities, your clients could have distinctive styles like VICE or Vox. Their voice tends to be more casual and conversational, something that speaks to many millennials, while newspapers target an older or traditional audience. Some digital outlets like first-person accounts of experiences—something that's difficult to find on the front pages of most newspapers around the world.

Armin Rosen—military and defense editor for the digital news organization Business Insider who has reported in either a freelance or full-time role from destinations like Cairo, South Sudan, Somalia, and Niger—says writing for the web can offer new writing styles and challenges more than traditional print outlets are able to do.

For instance, he once wrote a detailed, personal account of his experience at a pedestrian border crossing between the Gaza Strip and Israel. It included revealing insight into the border crossing's elaborate security measures and the demeanor of authorities stationed there.

"It was weirder and faster than I would have imagined it to be," Rosen says.

For journalists used to writing in protected air-conditioned newsrooms with comfortable work areas, the kind of on-the-ground reporting Rosen does could add valuable context to the coverage overseas at their target destination.

"It's a huge difference from office-based reporting," he says. "If you go to a place with a total open mind and curiosity, you'll see things that will give you richer insight in your reporting."

Rosen says just the state of the roads in a country can give you clues to the state of the government and the expectations of its citizens. Details like these can help strengthen your coverage of wider issues in a country.

"When I write about a place, I like to load it up with these details," Rosen says.

Digital news organizations that allow journalists to build their coverage using narrative-style reporting maximize their endless web space to allow stories to draw on the environments from which they are born.

It "conveys some sort of ground-truth," Rosen says.

Andy Beale, a freelance journalist now based in Albuquerque, NM, who spent two years reporting from Ramallah in the West Bank, values the space and freedom digital media provide.

"There's less length restriction," Beale says. "The space you have is only limited by what your editors think people will be interested in reading."

Also, don't ignore the ear. Practice writing not just for your eyes, but also for your ears. In broadcast writing, this is essential. It can sometimes be difficult for print reporters to switch gears and writing styles for broadcast. Most broadcast writing is in present tense, and active voice. For some news organizations, like NPR, listening to a report can sound like the story's journalist is talking directly to you.

Broadcast writing also allows plenty of room for sound. Whether it's television or radio, pieces often open with some kind of action that draws the audience in: gunfire in the streets of Ramadi, a missile launch in the Gaza Strip or crowds cheering after a hard-won election in Mumbai. The storyteller then usually incorporates the sound and action in the first few words of the story. Always write to what you see or hear. Place the listener or viewer at your location, draw them in, and maybe end with them feeling something—but always with a final quick summary or emotional sound bite.

Let's take a look at a radio piece from Marketplace's European Bureau Chief Stephen Beard:

> "London's Poppies prove the Value of Public Art"
> American Public Media's Marketplace® (p)(c) 2014. Used with permission. All rights reserved.
> By Stephen Beard
> November 11, 2014

> ANCHOR INTRO: This is the Marketplace Morning Report. I'm David Brancaccio. 11 a.m. Paris time on the 11th day of the 11th month, the First World War came to an end. It's Veterans Day here in the U.S. And this summer marked 100 years since the outbreak of hostilities that became what was then called the Great War. To commemorate Britain's war dead, an artist has staged a powerful installation at the Tower of London. It's really popular and lucrative for veterans' charities. Marketplace's Stephen Beard reports.
> [Natural sound of birds chirping and crowds]
> BEARD: This is a breathtaking sight: The empty moat around the Tower of London now runs red with a carpet of hand-made ceramic poppies. 888,246 of them have been hammered into

the ground. One poppy for each of the British and colonial soldiers killed in the Great War. So far more than four million visitors have come to shuffle past this unforgettable image of remembrance.

VISITOR: The fact that every one of these represents a death in the war begins to give some sense of the enormity of the loss.

VISITOR: Well, it's just an amazing way to commemorate the hundred years of the war. It's fantastic.

VISITOR: It's absolutely beautiful. It's stunning.

VISITOR: Very, very moving. Extremely moving.

BEARD: The memorial has had such an impact on Britons that there have been calls to turn it into a permanent display. But Nigel Hines, one of the organizers, says there's a problem with that.

HINES: Each of the poppies has been sold. And all the income from that has been donated to a range of charities.

BEARD: The sale of these ceramic poppies has raised around $25 million to help today's veterans and their families. Tomorrow the long process of dismantling the display will begin. A small selection of the poppies will stay in the moat until the end of the month, and then tour the country. But the rest will be shipped off to the people who bought them—mostly families of the war dead. The artist who created the display is ceramicist Paul Cummins.

CUMMINS: These people died for what they believed in. And the people who've bought them have relatives or a direct connection to them. So it completes a circle. They go home.

BEARD: Every day at dusk on the edge of the moat, an army bugler plays the last post commemorating the fallen. The poppies have to go says Cummins, not only to raise money for charity but also to symbolize transience. At the Tower of London, I'm Stephen Beard for Marketplace.

What I like about the piece is not only its simplicity, but how Beard quickly paints a scene—a challenge in radio where a listener has only their imagination to visualize places, people, and environments. Beard uses a few seconds of natural sound of chirping birds and milling crowds to open the piece. He finds a way to unobtrusively transport listeners to the Tower of London. He also describes the installation as running "red with a carpet of hand-made ceramic poppies. 888,246 of them have been hammered into the ground." It's such great imagery and not an outlandishly poetic piece as some young news broadcasters try to write.

Broadcast journalism can be a powerful medium. But it can be a challenge for many writers used to telling stories through print—and even digital media sometimes. But encouraging yourself to seamlessly hopscotch your way through the writing styles of every medium increases your personal value as a freelance foreign correspondent.

Certainly, this book does not aim to teach you journalism. It can't teach you how to write a newspaper article in the "inverted pyramid" method or how to craft a perfect broadcast lead. It cannot, because those fill the pages of many other valuable books. It only serves to remind you of the distinct challenges of writing in every medium to maximize your success overseas and your paychecks. I hope you'll explore multiple storytelling techniques to push your boundaries as a successful freelance foreign correspondent.

Your Papers, Please

Before you depart, you'll also need to gather up your necessary travel documents. Of course, you need a passport. But, you'll also need to begin the process early of applying for the appropriate visas to legally report and work from your target country. I explain more about considering the challenges of tough visa restrictions in a potential target country in the next chapter, but where you determine to go will affect how much time goes into securing the right visa for you.

Tunistra warns, "One of the things you must do before you go to a place is to have papers to support you."

Besides the obvious passport, gather up other things like your latest bank statement and your driver's license. Make copies of all of your important documents and cards, including your credit and ATM cards.

Also, go to a drug store and print out a few sheets of passport-style headshots of yourself. You'll need many of these. Although in many foreign countries, some subway stations have photo booths that allow you to take a quick headshot and print out several sheets of it for purposes like obtaining a discounted pass for public transportation. Store copies of your important documents in a safe location with you and also online in the Cloud or in your email to access them in case you need additional proof of identity and financial means for visa and foreign government accreditation. The copies can also be helpful if you lose something like your passport or your debit card is stolen.

Especially as a freelancer without powerful strings like the *New York Times*, working illegally as a journalist in a country like China without proper government accreditation can backfire quickly.

"In China, you could quickly get kicked out of the system easily," Tunistra says.

Beale says it's already challenging for freelancers to earn respect from official government channels, but even more so without government accreditation.

"As a freelancer it's particularly difficult to get access to official functions or official sources," Beale admits. "You're not as well respected I guess."

It's a different story for full-time foreign correspondents for well-known places like the *Guardian*. Government officials "kind of know they have to talk to you," Beale says.

So Beale decided to make the Herculean efforts to secure media accreditation while he was based in the West Bank, so he'd at least have a better shot of gathering reporting elements from authorities.

"I did eventually have to get media accreditation through Israel," he says. "I had to provide mountains of documentation to prove I was a working journalist."

He recalls making about 10 trips to the government press office and five trips to the interior ministry, with each visit requiring time-consuming border crossings.

"The Israeli government has some very strict limitations for who they give [press] cards to," says Beale.

But it paid off, not just with more access but also a legal chance to stay.

"The main benefit was I had an Israeli visa to stay there for the long-term," he says.

In some countries, having official government press accreditation allows journalists to apply for a residence permit and long-term visa.

Plan on devoting several months to arranging the proper work permits and your press visa from your home country—although in some cases, you may be able to enter your target country on a tourist visa and arrange for a press visa once you have arrived. It's best to start investigating this with the closest consulate or embassy of your target country.

You should also start working on getting a press pass to identify yourself as a member of the media. If you have managed to arrange strings before you leave home and have developed a strong relationship with an editor or producer, you might be able to secure a very valuable press ID with that organization. In some cases, they are worth their weight in gold. Flash a press credential from the *New York Times* or the BBC, and chances are you'll be able to get into many events you might not have even been credentialed for.

Working without a current and valid press ID from your news organization or a working press visa is possible. Nick Barnets gets by without either in Athens, although he does rely on an old CBS News ID from his days working for the broadcaster in New York. For him, going through the time-consuming challenges of getting official accreditation isn't worth the hassle, especially since he has a strong network of sources inside the government on whom he can rely to get information and access.

"Greece is a country where personal contacts go a longer way than a piece of paper or card," Barnets says.

However, I recommend applying to work in your target location legally, especially if you haven't ever stepped foot there before: which was my case in Turkey. It helps open doors for you to bureaucratic agencies, and the time intensive process can introduce you to authorities and officials who might be useful to have as contacts later down the line for information or to get access to high-profile newsmakers or politicians.

Another document you might be able to secure if you've found an interested and willing string: a letter of assignment. Often, this document is needed to secure foreign press visas and residence permits. But sometimes it's also requested when arranging for a press credential at a high-profile event. For example, even though I was approved to work as a foreign journalist in Russia, the Miss Universe Organization still requested a letter of assignment when I covered its Moscow competition for CBS Radio News.

The document should be printed on company letterhead and signed by a senior editor, producer, or news organization executive. It should describe in what role you will be working for the news organization in your target country. In some cases, like when I applied for a press card in Turkey, government officials will ask your news organization what kind of payment arrangements they have with you and how often they expect you will be paid. This can be tricky because it's hard to tell how fruitful any new relationship between a journalist and news organization will be on a freelance basis. See if general payment wording will satisfy authorities.

If your primary string is a little known news outlet or blog, ask your editor to detail where they are based, how government officials can review their work, and how big an audience they attract.

Don't feel hurt if a news organization won't immediately provide you with either their press identification or a letter of assignment—especially if you haven't even begun working in your target country yet. News organizations can be hesitant to put their name on the hook for a journalist with whom they aren't completely familiar. You may have to prove your usefulness and value to your strings once you're on the ground reporting, and then work out paperwork later.

Some journalism organizations also offer generic press passes.

If you join the National Writers Union and pay an additional fee, for instance, you can have a press card from the International Federation of Journalists delivered to your home with your picture, and translations of the card into several languages. It might not be helpful in securing a press visa from the UK, but it might be your only hope if you run into a surprise checkpoint by a local militia at the Ukrainian border—provided you have no other means of identifying yourself as a working freelance journalist.

If you aren't able to secure any of these types of documentation and identification, try getting the business card of your ambassador in your target country or another high-ranking embassy official. That shows you have already connected with the proper officials representing your home country, and their name might offer a little extra confidence in you from any hesitant foreign authority.

In Turkey, the government issued me a mustard-yellow press card that satisfied most of the credentialing requirements for covering official events and speeches. It also helped diffuse minor confrontations with police and authorities. However, don't always count on police being so friendly.

Press cards are worth the trouble in other ways as well. One of the most useful benefits of my Turkish press card was access to unlimited free rides on Istanbul's sprawling, hulking public transportation network that included subways, trams, a funicular, and even a cable car. As a freelancer on a modest budget, it was one of the best advantages of going through the hoops to get officially accredited.

But know when to draw the line. One time while working in Turkey the media accreditation office called me to ask if I wanted to join in on a free trip paid for by the government to Edirne to cover the legendary oil wrestling tournament. It's a popular sport in the country that dates back to the Ottoman Empire. It's often covered by curious media around the world, especially in travelogues. But accepting the government's offer would have put me in their pocket. I doubt my strings would have even accepted the stories I wrote because of ethical concerns had I divulged that important financial detail to them.

In other countries, the official government press card might even offer discounts and free tickets to events like soccer matches. But, again, don't neglect your role as an objective journalist—even if you see other journalists using these privileges. For the most part, I don't think you should take part in these offers.

Even if you're desperate, never pay someone or organization outright just for press credentials. Usually, it's unnecessary and wasteful. But, above all, don't abuse your media credentials or lend them to others. It puts your reputation and safety—along with those of other journalists—at risk.

Security Preparations

With regards to security, you'll want to register your travel with the U.S. State Department's Smart Traveler Enrollment Program (STEP). It's a simple online process that provides your contact information to U.S. officials should you get kidnapped or hurt while working overseas, and alerts you to security concerns.

Health insurance is another important consideration. If you already have health insurance, check to make sure it will cover you during your travels overseas. It's especially important to secure health coverage if you are going to a conflict zone.

Although Bach never visited a conflict zone during his time in Europe, he still purchased affordable basic traveler's health insurance for any unexpected emergencies.

"I had insurance just in case any unforeseen thing happened," Bach says.

Just a trip and fall on an ancient cobblestone street after a night of heavy drinking could mean costly medical bills, and perhaps a reporting trip cut short. Insurance helps protect you just in case.

If you have access to state-sponsored medical insurance that covers you at home, check to see whether there are reciprocal agreements in place with the government of the country from which you'll be based. This insurance you regularly use might also cover incidents abroad. Check with your insurance provider before you leave, because you might need to rely on travel insurance to fill in any gaps.

One private health insurance option you might qualify for is from Reporters Without Borders. Membership with the organization is required, but their insurance program offers worldwide coverage for any assignment; however, you'll have to pay more for coverage if you need it while in high-risk countries like Afghanistan, Iraq, and even parts of Russia. Travel.state.gov is a good resource to learn about the risks of an area you might plan to visit. Often, governments place countries like Syria on "high-risk" lists, which can affect whether insurers will cover travelers there, or if a traveler needs to purchase additional "war and terrorism coverage." This can be cost prohibitive.

You might also want to look into purchasing travel insurance. Journeying to far-flung countries is time consuming, expensive, and filled with potential problems. Travel insurance can offer an additional layer of protection on short- or long-term trips abroad.

I'd suggest World Nomads (worldnomads.com). They can be a bit pricey, but serious travelers recommend them and their policies are very comprehensive. World Nomads offers coverage for people from more than 150 countries, with coverage for medical evacuations, and 24-hour emergency assistance. The company's plans also offer coverage if your gear is stolen or damaged while traveling. If your $3,000 new DSLR camera goes on a permanent vacation from you to Guangzhou, when it's supposed to be in Nairobi, it might be good to have a way to replace it at little or no cost to you. Another insurance provider available online is International Medical Group (imglobal.com). This company offers a variety of plans tailored to suit nearly every type of traveler.

However, recognize, whenever you deal with insurance, especially travel insurance, that it can be painfully slow and complicated to file claims and receive reimbursement. In many cases, travel insurance providers require you to front any money to a hospital for an emergency visit in a foreign country, hopefully with reimbursement to follow. You'll also need to keep every receipt and document you have to back up your claim. And, unfortunately, it can take months to resolve a claim.

Language Learning

If you aren't already fluent in the language most widely spoken at your destination, you should start learning now. Borrow, or buy, as many books and multimedia resources as you can to introduce yourself to the language. You likely won't become fluent by the time you leave, but you'll have built a strong foundation for future learning after you've arrived at your destination.

Language-learning software like Rosetta Stone can be easy to use and helpful, but in my experience, they don't often teach you the mechanics of sentence formation, but instead focus on recognizing and remembering patterns.

Pimsleur is another popular option, and many language learners swear by it. It focuses on repetition to learn to speak, but not necessarily read or write, a foreign language. Pimsleur has been around for many years, and is often recognized for its audiotapes and CDs. These days the company also offers multimedia language learning options. I find Pimsleur to be helpful when trying to learn languages with unique speech patterns that are nearly impossible to learn through solely relying on text, like the four basic tones and fifth neutral tone in Mandarin Chinese and the sounds associated with Russian's Cyrillic script.

Some of these resources are available free at your local library. So take advantage of this while you can to focus on saving money for your reporting trip.

If you choose a location where you are completely unfamiliar with the language, try to connect with immigrants from that country at home prior to your departure. You'll be able to learn some informal or slang words that might be helpful in your newsgathering work overseas. They might also be able to guide you to more resources that could help your work once at your target destination.

If you expect to begin your reporting trip in a few weeks, realistically don't expect to make much substantial progress in learning your target language, unless you devote serious time to it. You will have to learn it more deeply once you are there. Visit local universities once you arrive and inquire about what language programs they offer for foreigners—in many cases, these are affordable and convenient. It's likely many of their language lessons also help you learn more about the location's culture, news, or politics. This is all beneficial to providing context to your own reporting.

It is *possible* to get by without even knowing the basics of the language spoken at your target destination. But this, clearly, is not to be recommended. But it's a reality whenever there are requirements for "parachute journalism." I discuss more about reporting in unfamiliar languages later in this book.

Fellowships and Grants

If you're worried about taking such a giant leap into the unknown consider a baby step. Plan a short visit to a country you are fascinated by. It could be as simple as a long weekend in Mexico City if you're a reporter in Phoenix. While you're there try to meet as many locals as possible, and generate story ideas. If you've got a seriously good, compelling story idea—that's enough to get the most skeptical editor at even the *Los Angeles Times* interested. And that's the most important part: if there are no stories, there is no hope.

Try to get a feel of the ease of reporting there, the challenges you might face, and the opportunities for storytelling. Are there Spanish-language media in the U.S. that want coverage from certain hometown areas of Mexico where they can't find a journalist? How do risks reporting along drug areas at the American border affect newsgathering?

Another opportunity to gain experience reporting abroad while still ensuring you have a safety net is the near endless number of fellowships, reporting awards, and grants available to journalists around the world. Some of the most respected programs include those run by the International Center for Journalists, the International Reporting Project, and U.S. State Department.

"As budgets are gutted at news organizations, people still need to report on the ground," says Melody Schreiber, Program Manager at the International Reporting Project run from the Johns Hopkins School of Advanced International Studies in Washington, D.C.

"That sort of coverage is absolutely crucial," she says. "Organizations like ours are helping to fill in the gaps."

IRP offers two types of programs for journalists from countries around the world: independent projects and group reporting trips.

The independent fellowships provide stipends and support to journalists proposing to report on a topic they choose generally anywhere from two to seven weeks in length at the target destination, although some projects have lasted up to three months. The journalist must arrange the logistics of the project overseas, including hiring fixers, drivers, and translators. However, IRP has contacts around the world that journalists may find valuable.

The group reporting trips pay for nearly all expenses of small groups of journalists to travel together to a target country to report on a theme. Many of the trips focus on underreported countries like Nepal, Ethiopia, and Tanzania. They also focus on underreported issues like health, nuclear security, and religion.

The journalists who take part in these opportunities are both freelancers and full-time staff at news organizations that range from traditional media like NPR to Mother Jones and blogs.

The IRP reporting programs give journalists "the opportunity to report with nuance and to really shed light on the subjects," even as newsrooms at home are stripped of money and time that can be devoted to in-depth reporting abroad, Schreiber says. Programs like these are important, because they fund reporting done thousands of miles away that could have a direct impact on the communities many news organizations like those in the U.S. serve, such as Latinos, immigrants, and American minorities.

Another Washington, D.C.-based non-profit, the International Center for Journalists, provides similar experiences and fellowships—many in partnership with the U.S. State Department and American embassies.

Most of ICFJ's programs target journalists in developing countries like Pakistan, but the non-profit does offer some limited opportunities for Americans and journalists in Western Europe.

"In this day and age when media organizations and journalists throughout the world are being asked to do so much more with less, and when the news space devoted to international news has shrunken so much, I think that these opportunities mean a great deal more to journalists from all over," according to ICFJ Proposal Development Director Robert Tinsley.

These programs offer opportunities to journalists at every level of their career.

"We're also able to offer experience for people who maybe have a little less experience reporting internationally—trying to make that leap into international correspondence," Schreiber said.

However, consider, both organizations report an increase in interest and competition for the opportunities they offer as more journalists seek work and experience in telling stories outside their home countries.

But there are many other opportunities available for journalists interesting in foreign reporting, especially those that provide financial assistance.

The *extremely* popular Fulbright National Geographic Digital Storytelling Fellowship is one of those opportunities. The highly competitive grant underwrites the costs of ambitious stories proposed by U.S. applicants at locations around the world. It allows for a full academic year of overseas travel and digital newsgathering and reporting in two to three countries. The fellowship is administered by the U.S. State Department and the National Geographic Society. It requires proposals fit within certain global themes like the environment, cities, and oceans. The application process is lengthy and exhausting, but the payoff can be substantial if selected. Digital storytelling training is also provided to fellowship recipients. Reporting produced during the project is featured on the National Geographic website. Previous fellows have been filmmakers, researchers, and artists and have focused on stories in Botswana, Cambodia, Mexico, the UK, and even Canada.

The Above the Fray Fellowship from NPR offers promising journalists the opportunity to cover underreported stories internationally. Applicants are selected based on proposals to report from a region that hasn't received much attention from the mainstream media. Fellows work for three months filing stories to the broadcaster for its radio and digital platforms.

Ultimately, there are many more fellowships, grants, and ways to fund your work abroad. You'll find many are targeted towards citizens of certain countries, reporters with specific backgrounds in beats like health or business, or encourage work in developing countries.

Many of these opportunities appeal to young journalists with just a few years of experience, but also big-name heroes of the profession who are looking for ways to fund new reporting projects. If you are in a position to take advantage of one of the opportunities, you should consider it.

A Self-Designed Future

Journalists chose to follow their career in foreign correspondence through a variety of ways. As you've seen from journalists so far, some went all in on working abroad completely on a freelance basis. Others found it more viable and financially sustainable to base themselves in their home country to make short trips overseas to pursue reporting opportunities they've arranged on a freelance basis before their departure. And some reporters choose to remain as full-time journalists at home, while taking advantage of fellowships and reporting grants that are also available to freelancers.

I believe the best reporting path for a journalist interested in foreign correspondence, but unable to find a full-time position reporting abroad, is to tackle the career path head-on independently. The risks are real. Not everyone will be successful. But it throws you into a churning sea of experiences that will transform not just your professional work and abilities, but also even your outlook on the world and life.

Regardless, whichever path you chose, all of these opportunities, suggestions, and ways to prepare for a career newsgathering overseas should occur months before you depart home. Give yourself time to save, say goodbye to friends and family, and start planting the seeds to independently find and successfully sell stories overseas.

Notes

1 Lewis, Jim. "NBC Bloommobile Page One," *GunTruck Studios*, 2004, http://guntruck.com/Bloommobile Page1.html.
2 Stelter, Brian. "For the Pullout, NBC Dusts off the Bloommobile," *New York Times*, http://tinyurl.com/qfxqbgx.
3 *Mercer 2015 Cost of Living Rankings*, 2015, https://www.imercer.com/content/2015-cost-of-living-info graphic.aspx.

2

CHOOSING A LOCATION

Now that you've determined why you want to work as a freelance foreign correspondent, you must consider the most important decision in how you'll do it: Where to go.

This is not a decision to take lightly—any decision you make will directly affect your success.

Professional Goals

In the previous chapter, we focused on not only why you want a new career as a freelance foreign correspondent, but also what you want to get out of it. Perhaps, like freelance photojournalist Carey Wagner, you're called to highlight human rights struggles around the global. Maybe, like Nick Barnets in Greece, you're fascinated by the new narrative of a county that has been close to your heart for your entire life. Or, like Andy Beale who started his career in freelancing in the Gaza strip, a complicated conflict with decades' worth of stories has caught your attention. However, you might have no interest in covering hard news on a daily basis: instead you might want to focus on writing feature stories on world cuisine, travel, and entertainment. Whatever your passion is, channel that into choosing the right location from which to begin freelancing.

Tailor your destination to your professional goals. If you want to concentrate on features, maybe Syria isn't the best location. Conflict journalism could be where your interests lie, but you won't get much of that in, say, Norway. So choose a location that easily enables you to pursue the kinds of stories you are most interested in covering.

But don't just pigeonhole countries into themes. Look for how ongoing story narratives around the world fit into your interests. For example, if you want to focus on human rights look past just basing yourself near the International Criminal Court at The Hague, and to the emerging stories of African and Middle Eastern refugees making the notoriously deadly trip across the Mediterranean to Italy and Malta.

See, your value on the market as a freelancer is your access to stories. Many news organizations already have journalists based in international hubs like The Hague and Brussels. Your strategy should be to fit yourself snugly into the new international jigsaw puzzle, complementing the coverage of existing stories but also telling new ones.

Accessing on-the-ground life and death drama allows you to sell your stories by supplementing the work of the journalists already reporting the nuts-and-bolts of your story's overarching theme. Those full-time staff journalists have access to researchers, and newsgathering resources that you might not immediately have at your disposal. So play towards your strength, which is original on-the-ground reporting and storytelling—something that can't be done from thousands of miles away.

A reminder of this premise is the scene in the 1982 movie *The Year of Living Dangerously*, based on the book of the same name, and starring Mel Gibson. A new foreign correspondent at his first post in Jakarta, Australian Guy Hamilton (Gibson) commits his first rookie mistake as a foreign journalist. He loaded his story up with dramatic political color reporting, but few facts. So, after filing his first radio dispatch on a crackly line to Sydney, his editor at home asks Hamilton: "Is that all?"[1]

Hamilton, exasperated in a hot and sweaty studio and defensive about his writing, responds: "What d'you mean? 'Is that all?'"[2]

"You could've written that from back here," his editor explains before matter-of-factly telling Hamilton, "that wasn't news, it was travelogue—get in there after the meat! Sydney out."[3]

As with real-life foreign reporting, adding color from a foreign destination is important, but facts are what pay the bills. Choosing a location that allows you easy access to newsmakers to get information that is much more difficult to get thousands of miles away is your competitive advantage, so milk as much as you can out of it.

In the pursuit of locating a destination that puts you at the heart of the stories on which you wish to report, be specific. For instance, don't just go to India because you want to cover poverty and human rights issues. Go there because you want to tell the stories of women who face the stigma of sexual abuse or how the increasingly high cost of living in Mumbai has left countless middle-class families homeless. Narrowing down your reporting interests will help you better craft a plan.

Think about the kinds of stories that fit within your theme and the advantages being in that location provides you to reporting on them.

"Find something that you want to do there: post-war Sierra Leone or the Americanization of Cuba," says Nicolas Axelrod, a freelance photographer based in Cambodia. He has long targeted specific stories that fit within his interests of human rights issues.

For freelance photojournalists, it's even more important that they have on the ground access to stories unfolding visually. Don't forget, most news services already provide endless stock photos of icons like the Pyramids of Giza. However, they might not provide the visual storytelling elements of nearby Cairo's crumbling infrastructure that's in such bad shape local leaders want to start fresh and just build a new city from scratch. When looking for ways to tell stories that have been done before, find a new take or angle that you can juxtapose with a theme or conflict at your location.

Also, find ways to "peopleize" your stories. Don't just tell your stories through the words of officials. Are there locations that provide you easier access to the real people behind the news or who are affected by it? Writing and photographing Kurdish Peshmerga soldiers fighting on the frontlines of their war against ISIS is much more powerful, and attractive to editors and producers, than focusing just on Kurdish commanders in their air-conditioned offices back in Irbil.

News

Now, if you actually want to make a living, you'll have to sell your stories. That means two things: there has to be enough news going on at your target destination, and it *has* to be interesting not just to you but to international markets, as well.

This is the most important financial consideration you'll have to make. It will determine whether your working and living plan at your target destination is sustainable.

But how do you know if your target destination is appealing to international markets or the audiences back at home?

Scour the newspapers, websites, and evening broadcasts to see whether your target country pops up at all, and, if so, how often. Also, set up a Google alert with the name of your country, city, or region. Monitor how often it pops up in news coverage—not just in local publications, but also in news outlets around the world.

There are some fascinating countries in the world that rarely get a mention in the mainstream media. For instance, Benin. The West African country sandwiched between Nigeria and Togo is one of the world's poorest countries, yet has one of the continent's most stable democracies. It has deep roots in Voodoo and its people were targets of the trans-Atlantic slave trade. The problem: the country might as well not even exist to the West. Its influence politically, economically, and culturally on countries like the U.S. is nominal. Except the occasional National Geographic feature story or human rights plea, Benin remains as mysterious to an American as Narnia does.

Tiny countries—especially in the South Pacific—like Nauru only seem to exist on a map as stopovers for Pacific island-hopper flights. The world's smallest republic isn't short on news, however. A financial crisis forced the government to sell off the country's assets to Australia, to pay a foreign debt. Now Australia pays the micro-country to detain the thousands of asylum seekers who try to make it to that continent. But the Nauru detention camps have been plagued with human rights concerns, including reports of sexual abuse by guards and poor living conditions. It's too bad the isolated nation fails to generate much interest from the restless searchlight because, for its size, it has a lot of potential.

On the opposite end of the economic spectrum another tiny country, Monaco, is a fabulous place to live in and even offers the occasional feature story on casinos and celebrities. But it faces continued international scrutiny for apparently tolerating money laundering and acting as a tax haven. But even this country, which sits at the doorstep of Europe, can't seem to get a break in the international media marketplace. So it might be hard to pay for all those yacht cruises and champagne breakfasts if you choose to base yourself in Monaco.

As you can note, the problem in these countries, and many others like them, is news sustainability. How much else is really going on in these countries that you could sell to news organizations around the world every single day—if not just on a regular basis? Even with the occasional "big" story like human rights and money laundering, news editors quickly tire of the same story—no matter how many different angles you offer. Unless these countries are part of a self-funded reporting trip, it will be a challenge to actually live and work there long term.

Getting Noticed

Like these often overlooked nations, there could be an endless number of intriguing stories to tell from your proposed country. They could all be visually stunning from a photojournalist's perspective. They could offer compelling color for newswriting or forecast larger issues at play for not just the country's region but also the entire continent! Your country could be the news jackpot you've been searching for. Or so you think . . .

Unfortunately, some international news markets rarely pay a second glance to entire swaths of the *world*. It doesn't even matter if there are meaningful stories there, because if it's not happening where the restless searchlight expects it to happen, it usually doesn't care.

The world's primary newsmaking regions are the Middle East, Europe, and Asia. These regions generally get a lot of attention from Western media because they have the military, financial, or historical interests of world powers like the U.S. and UK. But even many countries within these regions are neglected.

Countries such as Montenegro, Moldova, Kazakhstan, Oman, and Laos might as well be blank spots on a map for most American foreign news desks. Yes, occasionally there is a devastating natural disaster, violent riot, or international murder mystery involving an American tourist. The restless searchlight might cast a narrow and focused high beam on these places, but soon the international media storm moves on to the next disaster. Generally speaking, not enough news affecting power players in the U.S. and the UK happens on a regular basis in these countries to regularly command the attention of international media on a full-time basis.

I'd wager to say South America is the world's forgotten continent. It's largely ignored by many news organizations. Full-fledged news bureaus seem to be hard to come by in South America—especially since American news outlets can cover the continent when needed from hubs like Miami or even New York. This might be a different case for Spanish-language news organizations like Univision and news services like the AP and Reuters, but you certainly won't see much news from South America appearing on the front pages of many U.S. newspapers with as much regularity as stories filed from Iraq, Israel, and London. A visit from the Pope might spark attention or a mine disaster could grab the focus of the restless searchlight, but it's not often. Remember Uruguay? The small country pinned between Argentina and Brazil was a media darling when the world was first introduced to its colorful president when Uruguay became the first country to legalize marijuana in 2013. It also offered a glimpse of progress in South America when it legalized gay marriage that same year. But after that, the media lost interest. They didn't care much about the country's rampant cocaine addiction problems or its rise in violent crime. Instead, it was labeled a socially progressive haven and democracy by the international media, and the restless searchlight slowly faded away.

Elsewhere on the continent, stand-out one-off stories like the suspicious murder of a prominent and well-protected Argentine prosecutor that nipped at Argentina's president drew some attention. Before he died he was working on a case charging the president, Cristina Fernandez, with allegedly helping Iran cover up its purported role in a deadly bombing in 1994 targeting Jews in Buenos Aires. But, like many other South American stories, the limelight quickly faded.

Even Brazil—the epicenter of South America for international media—risks a voiceless future in international news once the Olympics in Rio de Janeiro are over, as the country's once booming economy stalls amid uncontrollable corruption and falling exports. Yet, even as the attention subsides, its struggles with poverty, crime, and environmental degradation will stick around long after the media center at the Olympics shuts down.

And, good luck finding almost any news from countries such as Guyana, Ecuador, Bolivia, and Paraguay. Their occasional pings on the news radar only act as reminders that these countries still exist to the outside world.

To the north, Central America has also fallen off a cliff. Once the news media left the region following the end of the Iran-Contra affair in 1987, the world left Nicaragua to sort out its own problems. In nearby Honduras and El Salvador, crippling drug trades, gangs, and emigration issues are certainly worthy of the world's attention yet barely get a mention. Today, even friendly, stable Costa Rica may be a draw for tourists but not for news crews.

With the exception of the occasional hurricane or earthquake, U.S. Caribbean neighbors like Jamaica, Bermuda, and even the American territory of Puerto Rico barely register on the news Richter scale. The most notable exception to all of this, of course, is Cuba. Once forgotten with the Cold War, the communist country has suddenly resurged with the energy of a sleeping child waking up on Christmas morning. The country has become a media superstar and offers a long-term beacon of hope for Caribbean news coverage.

Maybe the problem is the hemisphere, you ask. Well, take a look at America's northern neighbor, Canada. The friendly, peaceful country is one of the U.S.'s largest trading partners. But most Americans would probably be unable to locate Toronto or Montreal on a map. Like many other first-world countries, it's grappling with an influx of immigrants and a renewed threat of domestic terrorism. Yet through the eyes of most of its southern brethren, the most relevant things to come out of the country are Michael Bublé and Mike Myers. Perhaps the reason why U.S. coverage of Canada is so poor is because the country just isn't different *enough* to warrant the expense of newsgathering efforts there.

On the opposite side of the world, Australia—and especially its South Pacific neighbor New Zealand—is another example of a news dead zone to foreign audiences. Perhaps it's the stereotypes the country continues to struggle with in international media: a wild outback, home to friendly koalas and kangaroos where no news of significance happens, except the occasional piece on environmental threats to the Great Barrier Reef. However, news decision makers across the world are beginning to finally recognize the country's other stories: like Australia's struggle to prevent some of its own citizens from joining terror groups like ISIS, the increasing scarcity of water in parts of the continent, and its role in international trade—demonstrated when the country hosted the G20 in one of its fastest growing cities: Brisbane. New media, particularly BuzzFeed, have invested in operations in Australia. News from the country has a near daily presence on the site's U.S. homepage, even if it's only reduced to a listicle. Australia offers a glimmer of hope especially as a base to covering one-off stories in the South Pacific and natural disasters in lower Southeast Asia. Its flexible "working holiday" visa program also allows entrepreneurial young foreign journalists to work just about anywhere in the country for up to a year, which helps make the expensive country more sustainable. I used the visa program to work at a Brisbane radio news station as a producer to help subsidize my reporting for media back home.

Yet, there doesn't seem to be much hope for nearby New Zealand in gaining international attention, except when Christchurch was struck by a devastating earthquake in 2011. The friendly and quaint city continues to cope with the earthquake's effects years later as it wades through massive rebuilding projects in the destroyed "red zone" that has sealed off much of Christchurch's downtown. But I'd say even today despite the massive level of destruction to the South Island's second largest city, most Americans aren't even aware that there *was* an earthquake there. My guess is it happened around the same time the Arab Spring was taking over Tahrir Square in Cairo, and the attention of the restless searchlight was diverted to Egypt and the Middle East. Until the next earthquake, not much else seems to be happening in this peaceful, far-flung country that is often left off maps.

Even in Asia—a continent home to news powerhouse China, and gems like India and perhaps Burma—making a living on storytelling can be a challenge when you're off the beaten path.

Since 2008, Axelrod has worked to sustain a freelance photojournalism career in Cambodia. The country's deadly history with the Khmer Rouge, and its oppressive government with a poor record on human rights are certainly stories worthy of international news coverage. But it's been a challenge for Axelrod.

"There is not much that comes out of Cambodia news-wise," he says. "I just don't think there is a lot of interest."

Not only is it a struggle to flag down the short attention span of international media, but Axelrod also says the restless searchlight's intense international coverage of things like powerful earthquakes and political uprisings around the world dominate news cycles and ignore important stories happening in other places like Cambodia.

"They have space for that, and not space for Cambodia," he says.

However, in some sectors of the news, like finance and economics, non-traditional Asian newsmaking destinations thrive. Take Singapore and Kuala Lumpur, for example. The teeming cities draw considerable interest from financial news organizations like Bloomberg. Both cities are home to major banks and financial institutions. And in 2013, Bloomberg even opened a state-of-the-art office and studio in Kuala Lumpur to meet its increasing coverage needs of the regional and international financial center.[4]

The world even has a healthy appetite for travel news and some feature stories from the mega-cities as popular tourist destinations with access to world-class airports. But it might be a challenge to find and sell more mainstream hard news on a regular basis. Fortunately, with easy access to the rest of Asia, getting to big stories elsewhere in the continent can be quick. It's not as easy if you're based in more remote areas in Asia such as Mongolia or Laos and derive your income solely on enterprising and pitching story ideas.

North Korea is also a staple of international news coverage. There is no question that the world is fascinated with the country. And while it might not be feasible for most reporters to report *from* North Korea—it's certainly easy to report *on* the Hermit Kingdom from across the border in South Korea's capital, Seoul. South Korea is one of Asia's largest hubs, offering easy access to North Korean scholars at local universities, experts at human rights groups, and even North Korean defectors.

There is a seemingly insatiable appetite for North Korean news—even stories that would barely catch anyone's attention in any other parts of the world, like the Supreme Leader's love of cheese. And every so often the reclusive country makes international headlines firing missiles across the DMZ or launching something into space.

However, strict information controls from inside the country make it challenging to verify information. Most of the rhetoric from official North Korean government information channels from the country reaches levels of hyperbole, so it can be difficult to truly gauge sentiment there and among its leaders. Not only that, but there could be lulls in news coverage at times when the country is quiet and there is no way to enter the country to enterprise a more sustainable list of stories. Still, it represents a hearty beat for a freelancer who may also wish to cover news in South Korea at the same time.

You should also evaluate whether there is fatigue from most of the types of story that come from your proposed destination. For instance, stories about Syrian refugees huddled in masses along Turkey's border have been done. They have been done *many* times. Enough, well that's debatable. And this is not to say that the tragedy of these human beings is not tremendous and their effects on the Turkish government and the region are not enormous. This also doesn't discount the fact there is such a depth of sorrow in their personal stories that reporters haven't even begun to tell just a fraction of them Rather, in the eyes of most international media, they want something else. With no end in sight to the crisis, international media fear viewers and readers are tired of the same news from the same region.

"The conflict is dragging on," Brooklyn-based freelance foreign correspondent Zack Baddorf says. Editors are "going to be like, 'Ok, what's new?'" with more pitches on Syria.

While it's possible for you to partner with a NGO or human rights group to cover these important stories while generating another source of income, you might find it challenging to always find a place for your work in the mainstream international media marketplace by solely covering refugee stories in a single region like the Middle East.

But sometimes, on the other end of the news spectrum, certain destinations have a real potential for news market value, if you look past their initial coverage by world media.

Host cities for the Olympics and the World Cup are excellent examples of this. Most journalists outside Russia wouldn't give a second thought to searching for stories they could sell from Sochi. Why would anyone be interested in a hard-to-get-to mediocre summer resort that's often plagued by floods anyway?

Even many Russian journalists had long forgotten about the popular Soviet-era retreat, until it was named host city for the 2014 Winter Olympics. But as Sochi began to rise in name recognition, so did Russia and its prime minister-turned-president who ramped up his anti-Western rhetoric. Therefore, Sochi offered many story possibilities to international journalists beyond just the standard Olympics preparations and budget boondoggle old stand-bys. It served as an example of Russia's struggle with the rights of migrant workers who moved there to build the small city to international scale—a symbol of the country's relentless quest to regain its status as a world power. The coverage of Sochi even gently reignited some limited interest in regional security conflicts near the Caucasus that have long plagued Russia and slipped off the radar of international media.

Other events on the world stage like the 2022 World Cup in Qatar offer similar potential for enterprising journalists. Still years away, this World Cup has already been besieged with allegations of corruption—reaching as far up as FIFA itself. The event also faces serious human rights challenges for the immigrant workers who are building facilities there in the scorching heat, amid relentless demands. And there are always fears that ISIS and escalating regional instability could threaten to derail the whole games.

The challenge here for any journalist is trying to actually *tell* these stories. Qatar's government has no problem confronting, detaining, and expelling trouble-making journalists who probe where it doesn't think they should be probing. Already, the country has been on the offensive against many journalists who seek truth in a desert location where that's as hard to find as water.

When considering a location evaluate at the value of upcoming big events not just including the Olympics and World Cup, but also decisive elections, international conferences like the G20 and the potential for the death of a popular or controversial aging or ill government leader or monarch.

Forecasting News

You also want to look beyond predictable sources of upcoming news like events. In essence, you must accept the news potential of a particular location as a game of chance. But you must work to rig it in your favor. You must make some sort of news prediction. The best success you can set yourself up for is choosing a location that quickly becomes an international media star—before most people realize it. Then, you'll have the edge on other journalists competing against you because you'll already be in position when strings start calling.

Balint Szlanko, a freelance foreign correspondent based in Hungary, admits that choosing to work in any country before it becomes the focus of the international media's intense restless searchlight is a bit of a crapshoot: "I think there is an element of luck," he says.

It's almost as if you're choosing a stock. You must gather a bit of information on key indicators of news potential and then get in on the ground floor.

A prime example: Ukraine. Once one of Europe's quietly rising stars, it's become a tug-of-war between the EU and its Soviet past. The journalists who were able to spot early protests in Kiev as something more than just run-of-the-mill anti-government demonstrations and recognize Russia's influence on the country were on the ground already in position when Putin's (alleged) tanks came rolling across the Crimean border. Those journalists cashed in, while reporters from around the world were still trying to figure out a way into Crimea, and where and how to report on the quickly evolving dynamics of this real-life game of Risk unfolding before the world's eyes.

Szlanko says he did head off to Ukraine to report on the early protests in Kiev but, like many other journalists, he didn't expect them to have much of a shelf life and stick around: "I wasn't interested in covering street clashes," he says. "I don't think anyone realized it would turn into an international affair."

Cuba could fit into a similar category. There were few indications that the U.S. would normalize relations with the communist island nation after more than 50 years. Then, suddenly, in December 2014 all of that changed when President Obama announced his efforts to repair diplomatic ties with Cuba and its president Raul Castro—brother of the infamous guerrilla leader, Fidel.

The move was a surprise to even the most celebrated experts in Cuba–U.S. policy. And it set off an early economic transformation of Havana—cut off from the world for decades, yet just 90 miles from Key West, Florida. The changes to Cuba are just starting to happen. But already interest in Cuba from Americans has soared.

Tour companies have been capitalizing on "intrepid" Americans who want to visit Cuba. Cruise lines are planning visits to the island and the modern world is crashing through its front door. Diplomats are rushing to resume work in new embassies in each of the country's capitals. And large populations of Cuban-Americans, especially in south Florida, are taking notice of the controversial diplomatic engagement with the country their families once fled.

All of this has caught the attention of the American news media. The once sleepy outpost of a relative handful of news organizations like CNN and CBS were jolted awake. And other broadcasters, newspapers, and online news media are starting to invest again in Cuba, more than 25 years after the end of the Cold War.

The journalists already in Cuba are seizing on the country's new relationship with the U.S. The journalist accreditation process can be challenging, and communications and newsgathering logistics can be just as daunting. So the journalists there who have already figured it all out are seeing a future paved with news.

The benefit of this story for a freelance journalist is that it's not just a one-and-done event. It's not like the U.S. decides to be an engaging neighbor with Cuba again, and everyone goes on with life, and the restless searchlight moves on. While the focus on the story isn't as intense as when President Obama's decision was first announced, there continues to be significant interest in its ongoing effects.

For instance, what will the eventual access be to the country for American tourists? Sure, they can visit now for "cultural exchanges," but when will they be able to arrive on a direct flight from New York with only their passport and their wallet open for the first Cuba Libre outside the arrival gates? How will this influx of attention and outsiders affect the country, its people, and its economy? And when will the U.S. trade embargo of Cuba end? When can Americans legally buy Cuban rum and cigars at home? And how will that affect the American companies trying to compete in the same market with the same products? But, most importantly, will a taste of a more open government and direct relations with a first-world democracy and economic powerhouse lead to political change in Cuba? Could we see then end of the Castro regime and maybe the end of communism there altogether?

The steady flow of news from Cuba allows each of these stories to be tackled one at a time. But, the wise freelance foreign correspondents are already there. They're able to milk the news cow at a steady pace, not drying it up all at once. And at this point, they might even be full-time staff.

While getting in on stories like Ukraine and Cuba early on might just be pure luck, recognizing other news generators around the world isn't.

Evaluate a broad range of newsmaking elements that have global impacts—especially if they affect the West.

What threats do communicable diseases like Ebola, SARS or Zika have on your proposed destination? Are they global hubs with direct access to many other countries? Is a coup in a key U.S. ally in a troubled region on the horizon? Is a rumbling volcano near a densely populated city threatening to pop? Is a controversial, powerful, colorful, and mysterious leader emerging in a country that captivates the attention of the West, like Kim Jong-un?

In many senses, you're not just doing a surface-level analysis of emerging events and story themes in an area, you're evaluating them on an abstract level. You're looking for far-reaching cultural shifts, a sputtering economy, and a government on the verge of collapse or the failure of a country's relationships with its neighbors and the rest of the world.

Deep stuff, huh?

This is no easy task—recognizing the potential for news before anyone else does. But, hedging bets and investing in the stock market aren't any easier, although they'll certainly get you richer.

There are some pitfalls to gambling on whether a city, country, or region will make it big.

Avoid forecasting too far into the future.

As an inexperienced young journalist new to freelance foreign correspondence, the very first country I wanted to zero in on was the Philippines. Just before I began to consider my potential move to Manila, the Obama administration announced its "pivot to Asia." It's sort of a repositioning of military and economic strategies into the Pacific to counter the growth of China. I believed the Philippines would be the new frontier of international journalism as the pivot took shape. I saw a U.S. military base poised for growth within close proximity to China that would allow Americans to more easily fight back against Chinese aggression in nearby disputed territories and waters, and defend its allies and interests in the region.

The U.S. wars in Afghanistan and Iraq were winding down, and analysts were beginning to search for what was on the horizon for American foreign policy. The thought was that the U.S. would shift its focus from the Middle East to the Pacific and reposition its navy resources to accommodate this new change in economic and security priorities. China had become the world's second largest economy and nearby North Korea continued to provoke world concerns.

Then, the Middle East blew up. The Arab Spring revolutions began to fall apart. The promise of a progressive democratic future for North Africa and the Middle East evaporated. Terrorists took the places of deposed leaders. Syria fell farther into chaos and pulled Iraq down with it, once the safety net of thousands of American troops stationed there unraveled. The influence and barbarism of ISIS reached across continents and the Mediterranean and began to inspire terrorism concerns as far away as Australia. At the same time, the U.S. and world powers began to ramp up their years' long negotiations on preventing Iran from building a nuclear weapon.

However, as Fareed Zakaria noted in his April 2015 *Washington Post* column "Whatever Happened to Obama's Pivot to Asia?"[5] the Middle East became just too much of a distraction to the U.S. to allow the country to dedicate most of its attention elsewhere.

Right now, the U.S. is still interested in engaging Asia. It is following through with some of the elements of its pivot. Renewed trade and economic negotiations, visits to Asia from high-ranking officials including President Obama, and strengthened alliances with Pacific nations like Vietnam and Japan show the U.S. still considers the continent a vital component of its foreign policy. But the day still hasn't arrived when Asia becomes the country's foreign policy centerpiece.

In the long term, it's definitely possible the U.S. will continue to invest resources and attention into Asia. But with the resurgence of Middle Eastern emergencies, my mistake was thinking I could capitalize on the pivot so soon. This is a national strategic shift that likely won't result in many concrete changes for at least several years, if not decades.

My error became even clearer when I contacted journalists in Manila. They offered little hope that the pivot would offer many immediate news opportunities. They also complained about widespread neglect of the Philippines by American media, except for the occasional tropical cyclone. I needed to make money immediately . . . not in 10 years' time.

Learn from my initial failure. Trying to forecast news trends too far into the future overlooks what you need to really focus on, which is what's coming up next, soon, and how can you get in before everyone else? You should probably focus on the next three months to two years.

Another foxhole of failure is trying to link a city's population to its potential for news in the *international* market. Mexico City is one of the world's most populous cities. But, you'd hardly know that if you lived in the U.S., because most stories from Mexico focus on drugs and cartel violence along border towns. They're usually not on thriving cultural and art scenes typical of similarly sized cities or even politics. Mexico City has tons of other news of interest at a local level, but it's hard to wave over the media next door to even take notice unless it's related to "El Chapo." Iraq's former ISIS stronghold-turned-ghost town of Ramadi has more international coverage than Mexico, a world away.

Our long neglect of Mexico may never have been more obvious until in October 2015 monster category five Hurricane Patricia slammed into the country's Pacific Coast, just south of the popular tourist resort destination of Puerto Vallarta. The storm's rapid transformation into a potentially devastating hurricane caught news organizations by surprise. With news bureaus there, reporters scrambled from the U.S. to make it to airports in the storm's path. By that time, however, they were already shut down.

U.S. broadcasters especially needed to be there to get live video of the hurricane's landfall. Unable to get there, most relied on hotel webcam live streams and phone interviews of people who were evacuated. However, many organizations, including CBS News, turned to freelancers in Mexico to help fill coverage gaps.[6] Yet the slim coverage was obvious and embarrassing for U.S. media.

Even popular and populous world cities like Paris, Madrid, and Munich sometimes struggle for attention. The evolving regionalism of Spain and the shifting cultures and ethnicities of Paris can't compete with gory ISIS beheadings. As a result, many legacy news organizations have closed once key bureaus there. Although they still offer the potential for intriguing feature stories and easy access to other news-making events in the region, finding strings interested in the stories there on a daily basis will be a challenge, especially for new freelancers. Perhaps one exception to this is Rome, where the walled Vatican has become a fortress of news. While the Pope has always been a key figure in news, it's hard to remember a time when the leader of the church was as capable of drawing the interest of world media—often in a positive way—as Francis does today.

First-World Terrorism

Terrorists have become masters of media. Indeed, they are successful navigators of social media. They recruit followers on Twitter and Facebook and they spread their messages of hate with the simple click of a mouse. But they are also professional public relations agents for their terrorist organizations.

They recognize that their deadly tactics are far less impactful in Western media if they take place in Pakistan or Afghanistan. Western media are accustomed to seeing terror reports in those countries. Let's be honest, you know—the standard deadly market explosion story. So extremists are targeting their acts of fear in locations that have a direct impact on the West: Tunisian beaches popular with sunbathing Brits, Parisian streets, and tourist attractions and mosques in Middle Eastern U.S. allies such as Kuwait.

What this means for you, when selecting a target destination, is to consider how your proposed location has been affected by international terrorism. Or if it looks positioned to be vulnerable to a terrorist attack.

Terrorism is universal. A deadly terror attack involving Westerners will get airtime and newspaper space around the world. But it has also transformed the dynamics of foreign news. While it's difficult to divert the attention of cash-strapped American news agencies from the Middle East, to perhaps Amsterdam to cover the city's cultural landscape—media will immediately snap awake to an ISIS bombing in a touristy neighborhood there.

This has recast some destinations that have struggled to get a share of the restless searchlight as news-making locations because of terrorist activities, security threats, and police raids.

Consider how terrorism affects your proposed location because it could be a sustainable source of stories. While it's hard to forecast domestic terrorism, there could be indicators that international extremists could be worrying the leaders of the country you're targeting.

How is the government responding to terrorism at your target destination? How are these threats shaping border security, the economy, and tourism there? And, most importantly, why are terrorists attracted to this country, city, or region? Are there systemic breakdowns in society that allow or inspire homegrown terrorists? What's the country's stance on immigration? And how is the country working with international partners like the U.S. and the UK to relay threats to those allies to fight terrorists? One-off minor terrorism events in otherwise dull countries won't be worth much to you. But if they become a recurring issue then it might transform into a sustainable location from which to report.

Decades ago most terrorism was localized: IRA in Ireland, ETA in Europe's Basque region along the Spain–France border, and the Tamil Tigers in Sri Lanka. Today, the reach of ISIS and al-Qaeda inspires terrorists and extremists around the world. As a foreign correspondent, you must recognize the influence and effects of terrorism to better respond to it as a journalist. Consider this in your decision when choosing a location in which to base yourself.

Competition

There's no easy way to say this: Expect cutthroat fierce competition as a freelance foreign correspondent. You're up against well-paid full-time foreign correspondents, local journalists with the same connections you have to media organizations back home and other foreign freelancers. Everyone is competing for stories and paychecks. This means you must carefully consider the current competition landscape wherever you plan to go.

Bradley Secker, a freelance foreign correspondent based in Istanbul, says competition there has increased over the last four years. Despite what he describes as friendly competition, he admits the city has become more crowded with journalists.

"We are all a big family of freelancers and staffers somehow, but we are also competitors," he says of the increasingly crowded community of journalists in Istanbul. "One day we will be drinking beer together, and the next we will bump into each other at the latest breaking news event somewhere."

But Bridgette Auger, who freelanced as a documentary photographer based in Beirut, says the competition there was much less than it was in her previous location, Cairo: "As a photographer, I didn't feel like the market was overly saturated with photographers based in Beirut," she says. Because, "There are people who live there and work around the region."

That means fewer people were competing directly with her in Beirut, only really using it as a base from which to report elsewhere across the Middle East.

Despite whatever competition exists for news and strings, Auger, like Secker, acknowledges that the community of local freelancers can often come to the rescue of others: "Treat your fellow freelancers (and staffers) well and they will take care of you in return," Auger says. "The community is quite small and if someone can't take a gig they will pass it along."

You might also "form a relationship with a writer from an outlet and if you work well together they will try to bring you along," she says.

Other regions such as Southeast Asia, continental Europe, and the UK can also be competitive for journalists. Most of these locations serve as hubs for newsgathering in large parts of the world. These hubs can be flooded with more full-time journalists, where your services aren't needed.

The level of competition sometimes even depends on your beat or medium. If you join, a rising tide of photojournalists chasing their wanderlust and snapping images of poverty or temples in India you could drown in competition. While a freelance journalist focused on less glamorous regulatory news of interest to global financial markets and multinationals with Indian operations might be cashing fat paychecks every month. It all varies on what kind of news you're targeting and for whom.

Get in touch with as many full-time and freelance journalists as you can while deciding on whether to pursue a career at your target destination. To evaluate competition among journalists at a destination, work on getting answers to the following questions: Do freelancers there get much work? Are there any star journalists who seem to be featured in many news outlets that have a monopoly on the market? Is there enough news available in your target destination to support the current freelance market there? And, perhaps most importantly, are there segments of the market with potential for growth, like financial journalism?

You might not be able to get all of these questions answered prior to your arrival, but you'll have enough information to make a more informed decision on whether it's worth your time and money.

But don't always expect all freelancers to help you out. They don't want to encourage others to jump into the market and make it even more competitive for them, and everyone else already there.

Costs

Besides considering your target destination's value to the international news market, you should also examine the cost of living in your location. We pointed to this in the previous chapter. But choosing somewhere that requires extraordinary expenses to live and work in will pressure you even more to start churning out content that you will get paid for. This might either be a motivator to get your shit together, or a distraction to your career.

Hopefully, you'll arrive at your destination with a substantial amount of savings. That will help ease your transition into your new location. But, depending on where you go, you may need more savings accumulated before you arrive at your proposed location.

Here's a handy general rule of thumb for weaving your way through the world on a budget: the quieter the country, the more expensive it is. Cairo, for example is loud, chaotic and often packed with news. And, fortunately, for the correspondents based there, it's relatively affordable. But at the opposite end of the spectrum are places like Iceland. While the country could offer unique opportunities to report on the environment and climate change, the cost of living and working there will make you want to rush back to the airport for the next flight out. The same is true for other peaceful countries like Norway, Sweden, and even the UAE.

There are many factors to consider when you're evaluating a location's cost of living and working.

The most immediately noticeable cost can be just obtaining a press visa. Countries with tightly controlled media like China and Russia come with a steep visa price for freelance journalists. Just the privilege of entering these countries as a working journalist can cost you hundreds of dollars. Not to mention the cost of your time spent devoted to navigating the visa process.

Even in Turkey, while the cost of a press visa isn't outrageous, the bank deposit amount required for a residence permit was. The Turkish government required proof that a residence permit applicant had enough money to live there without having to be a burden on the country. Therefore, the application for the permit asked for a Turkish bank statement showing evidence of funds in your name in Turkish lira. However, just opening a local bank account as a foreigner there should be declared torture. So the other option was to go to a currency exchange office and bring the government a receipt that showed you exchanged the sufficient amount of money into Turkish lira. But really, who's going to carry around a briefcase full of thousands of dollars' worth of Turkish lira—especially with the risk of the currency collapsing. So as a result, many foreigners were able to bribe the currency exchange manager for a fake receipt that showed the appropriate amount of Turkish lira that they could bring to the government to complete the application.

This, of course, isn't the wisest idea. It could put you in jail and send you home. It could also end up costing you much more than you bargained for. Folks who have ended up in overseas prisons, even on minor charges, have horrific and expensive stories to tell. I cannot recommend doing things like this to make the possibility of living and working in a foreign country easier. You should make every effort to follow the law. Don't take shortcuts that could offer you a way to save time or money, but could also end up costing you much more in the long run.

Now, once you've made it in and can stay for the long term, you also have the expenses of actually living there. You might have to stay in a hostel immediately on your arrival, if you don't have any connections in the country to help arrange accommodation for you. Generally, cheap hostels are available in most parts of the world, especially in Southeast Asia. In Vietnam, you'll easily be able to score a hostel for just a few bucks a night, and it might even come with a small daily breakfast. But in London and Paris, you'll likely pay 10 times as much per night, without even a piece of toast included in the price. While in yet other locations, such as Stockholm and Moscow, affordable hostels are even harder to find, which might force you into staying in an expensive hotel. After a few nights, you'll begin to notice how the costs quickly add up. Staying in hostels for any extended period of time can also become a distraction. Try doing work while a couple of your drunken roommates are going at it in the bunk bed above you.

After you've arrived in a city, you'll also have to find affordable transportation. My recommendation: choose a location that has a strong and affordable public transportation network. Cities like Lisbon and Bangkok offer competitive rates on taxis, but other destinations like Sydney can be much more challenging for a frugal freelancer. To manage costs, you'll want access to subways, trams, monorails, and buses to get around. Cities with extensive and reliable public transportation include Istanbul, Kuala Lumpur, Singapore, Hong Kong, Tokyo, Madrid, and Berlin. If you plan to report often from across the region, consider whether your target destination has public transportation available to the airport—these can easily be the costliest trips in taxis.

Now, the largest part of your budget: rent and food. Living in a large apartment in Buenos Aires, Tokyo, London, or Melbourne can cost you thousands of dollars per month. As a freelancer, you'll need a location that's close to downtown areas so you can easily access government offices, public transportation, businesses, and news conferences. In most cities, not much happens in the suburbs. But living in, or close to, downtown will also drive up the cost of your apartment.

To fight soaring rents, find a roommate. Craigslist is used in many countries, but more popular alternatives like Gumtree are also available in countries like the UK and Australia. Check with local journalists to determine how they find affordable housing—especially online. In some hostels where travelers stay for weeks, foreigners or locals will post notes on bulletin boards alerting travelers to open rooms. You could also have some success getting in touch with the local foreign correspondents association. In Istanbul, it's simply a free Yahoo group listserv. Members of these groups can offer some valuable guidance, especially for people trying to find roommates or share accommodations. Groups like these also offer the most current advice when dealing with the quirky and fast changing process of obtaining residence cards and press visas.

Ultimately, however, you might find yourself sharing a one-bedroom apartment with two other foreigners if you are in an expensive city. It might not have to be permanent though, so try to be optimistic.

If you have friends or family in a country, don't be too proud to ask for their help or their couch—at least while you get settled.

Wherever you settle, however, ensure you have access to a quiet space. It'll be difficult to edit audio when your musician roommate is having has his jam band over every evening. Besides making it a challenge to concentrate on work, it will sound unprofessional if you're trying to communicate with clients on the phone while your roommate is watching *Mad Max* in surround sound in the room next door.

Once you've found a place to stay in, you'll need to find fast reliable internet. That's not a problem in Seoul or Hong Kong. But it is quite a test in remote areas of the Middle East or Africa. Finding internet access is essential. If you plan to work in radio, you might have to Skype with a string on super-short notice. Or you might need access to email to receive and send things needed to quickly file a story. If you're working with video, you'll need a way to FTP large files.

Always relying on internet cafes and public hotspots is too much of a gamble. Sure, they're valuable in a pinch and can cut down on your smartphone's data usage, but during peak usage times they can be slow and unpredictable, and access can be intermittent. You also make your personal and professional data vulnerable to hackers. Having regular access to a reliable internet connection allows you to be connected wherever and whenever a string needs you.

But even when you do have regular reliable access to the internet, it might not be as fast and affordable as it is back home. In the U.S., cable and fiber optic Wi-Fi is plentiful and generally affordable. But, even in developed countries, many households rely on slower ADSL connections that might offer spotty service. So, as a backup, try to get a local voice and data plan for your smartphone. We discussed how to select the right mobile phone options prior or just after you arrive in your target destination in the previous chapter.

Of course, you'll also need access to reliable power. But if you're in a city where just finding power is a struggle then there are many more priorities on your list than internet.

Of lesser importance, but definitely a significant portion of your budget, will be food. Hanoi, Hong Kong, and Beirut all offer cheap and filling street food. But elsewhere, a basic sit-down burger and fries at a bar can cost upwards of $20 in Perth, say, or Queenstown. Add on a beer—or two—and you've just burned through a wad of cash for the day.

If you don't know how to cook already, learn now. Of course, if you're a gourmet and living in Almaty, you might have some trouble trying to track down groceries such as Brie, spaghetti, tuna fish, or even some basic American staples like peanut butter. And, if you do, expect to pay a premium for food that isn't a regular part of the family diet at your target destination.

You might also *love* tikka masala. But think about eating tikka masala, or things very similar to tikka masala, every day. EVERY. DAY. You might quickly begin to hate it. Sometimes, just having a simple homemade bacon cheeseburger is a luxury. Gathering together all the ingredients to make that, in a place where meat—especially pork—isn't popular can be costly. But sometimes, it's worth it. Try to learn how to cook what's cheapest and most readily available where you are. Then, save your favorite meals from home as an occasional treat.

At the bottom of your list of expenses is finding affordable clothes, and being able to afford that occasional night out without having to worry about going bankrupt. I think most Americans take for granted how cheap these expenses are for them. Our "Made in China" clothes are a bargain for foreigners who come with empty suitcases just to fill up before they return home. And an evening out can also be a bargain compared to in many other Western countries.

Now, all of these expenses are magnified and expanded if you consider living and working in a conflict zone.

In these dangerous locations, you'll need to buy or at least rent additional equipment including a costly flak jacket (a form of body armor) and a proper helmet. Just those two essential elements of protective gear for news reporting in conflict zones can cost hundreds of dollars.

In severely devastated or remote areas, affordable temporary accommodation options will also prove to be scarce—because they simply don't exist. That's the case along many parts of the border between Turkey and Syria. So, you'll have to shell out money for either an expensive hotel or arranging for a driver and staying with a local family or friend. This all greatly adds to the logistics of trying to report from—or even near—a war zone.

At the same time, you're trying to compete against the large daily budgets and per diems of full-time foreign correspondents who have also been dispatched to the same location for the same story. There's just no way you can pay the same rates for fixers and drivers as they can. It's just hard to compete financially. We zero in more on the challenges of living and working in areas affected by wars and conflicts later in this book.

Finally, if you believe you might have trouble making a livable income at a location, consider working on the side. This could mean freelancing at a news organization such as the *Lebanon Star*—an English-language newspaper that's provided a lifeline to many freelance foreign correspondents in Beirut for decades. You might also consider teaching English—a path that's particularly popular in Asia. But new government policies in some countries can make this a difficult endeavor for unqualified foreigners.

"I've done all kinds of odd jobs to support myself as a freelancer, I even did real estate in Beirut," says Auger.

But, beware; working on the side can be a distraction to your work as a foreign correspondent if it takes up too much of your time.

Still, adding all your living and working costs up lead to a significant total. So, based on your current personal financial situation, you might find it more financially practical to start off in an affordable destination.

In Cairo, Auger found that the city was "much less expensive than Beirut so your money goes further."

Wherever you go, the cost of living and working in a location will have a direct impact on your success as a freelancer. Only working one day a week goes much farther in Vietnam than it does in Canada. Choosing a location with long, slow periods of newslessness and high costs of living and working is a recipe for failure.

Ease of Reporting

How easy will it be to actually report in your proposed destination?

First, you should evaluate your language challenges. If you've already decided on a destination, you should have already gotten to work by now learning its primary language. Resources for achieving this are discussed in the previous chapter.

However, here's a secret: *mastering* the local tongue isn't as paramount in some destinations as it is in others.

In Spain, for instance, most news is written and spoken in Spanish. So are government documents and press releases. And many Spaniards can be shy about speaking English, even though they might be perfectly able to. But Spanish isn't all that hard to learn—especially in contrast to other languages. So even just learning a little Spanish can go a long way in getting people to open up.

The same is true in areas farther east. Honestly, I struggled to learn Turkish. I did all the right things: I lived with a local Turk who could speak barely a few words of English, I surrounded myself with Turkish newspapers and other news media, and I enrolled in an online Turkish language class at a prominent Istanbul university. But my problem was I was lazy. When I had the opportunity to speak English with friends or while working independently, I did. And the online course was too flexible to force me to sit down and learn every day, like an intensive in-person class would have been.

So I hit a wall with my Turkish abilities. I could generally recognize words and verb forms, but had trouble putting it all together. So my de facto introduction in Turkish on the telephone was: "Hello. I am a journalist. Do you speak English?" Often, they'd reply with "yes," or put me on hold while they'd look for someone. This can be an obstacle to getting facts and information, especially under deadline. However, as in many other countries where English isn't the first language, business operations, conferences, media briefings, and press releases are often in English.

In some cases, you might get by on a language that isn't the primary one in your country. For instance, if you are living and working in Vienna, you might be able to work in French and English, rather than Austrian German. That's because many international organizations with offices in Vienna, including the UN, operate in several languages. Major businesses and high-profile public figures also speak several of these core languages.

It can be much more challenging, however, in countries where it's not that way. Russia, China, and Japan all fall into this category. The benefit of speaking, reading, and writing languages there fluently means better understanding of those countries and the dynamics in them. But these languages can also be tough to learn—especially for those inexperienced with language learning. They have strange characters, sentence structures, and idioms. You may occasionally work on an assignment where all of your sources and interviewees speak English, but you'll still need the help of friends, fixers, and translators who speak the local language to tackle most other stories. This is especially important if you're out on the street trying to talk to "everyday people," where stopping them and asking if they speak English will be a major pain in the ass for both you and them. If your heart is set on these countries, it's best to spend much more time before you depart working on your language abilities.

Anger's advice: "Learn the local language and hang out with local people. Don't get stuck in the bubble of journalists or expats. Read lots of books."

Also, never rely on language translation apps or software. Apps like Google Translate might be effective at getting the general idea of foreign news releases and website content, but don't trust them to translate quotes or paraphrases you'll include in your reporting. They're often wrong. Not necessarily because they translate a text inaccurately, but because they lack the context with which it came. A computer translation might miss key subtleties like connotations, and tone that are important to accurate interpretations. Or maybe a word has multiple meanings. A human translator can more accurately fine tune this to produce more reflective and precise quotes and paraphrases. But relying on humans will cost you money. If you do ask a translator for help, pay them. Don't just ask for favors. I believe you should even pay your friends and colleagues who put in time to help you translate.

Another important factor to consider while gauging your ability to report with ease is your freedom as a journalist.

The Committee to Protect Journalists annually releases a list of the countries that arrest the most journalists. The worst repeat offenders: China, Iran, Eritrea, Egypt, Syria, Myanmar, Ethiopia, Vietnam, and even Turkey.[7] Many of these countries are, of course, ruled by oppressive regimes or are failed states. Worldwide, hundreds of journalists are in jail just for doing their jobs. The power of the pen is a threat to many governments. Most of the journalists in jail are locals. But there are foreigners among those behind bars, or awaiting a trial. Some of the most prominent journalists caught up in foreign courts were four journalists with Al Jazeera who were among those arrested in Egypt and imprisoned for terrorism-related charges following their reporting on the Arab Spring, before they were eventually released. And it was only after more than 500 days in an Iranian prison on espionage charges that the *Washington Post*'s Tehran Bureau Chief Jason Rezaian was released after months of secret talks with U.S. negotiators.

In a 2015 interview on Al Jazeera America, former *New York Times* correspondent Nazila Fathi recalls being threatened while she reported during the 2009 uprising in Tehran.

Fathi says that "People close to the government" there even called her and threatened to shoot her just for covering the protests.[8] The situation got so bad that, once her apartment building came under "surveillance," she was forced to leave the country.

But it's not just the threat of jail time that governments use to intimidate journalists and silence the press. Some foreign reporters and photojournalists also find their visas denied or cancelled, as has been the case in China.

In 2013, China delayed the issuances of journalist visas—causing U.S. Vice President Joe Biden to intervene during a trip there. He chastised the country's leaders for refusing to say if they were going to renew the visas of some correspondents and for shutting down access to American-based news media that are often critical of China's leadership, according to the *New York Times*.[9]

That year, China rejected a visa application from a reporter who had waited eight months to start a new job with Reuters. The veteran reporter had covered Asia for decades, including Beijing, for other news organizations.[10] The country did not offer an explanation. Mooney relocated to Rangoon in 2014.

The pressure by the Chinese government has apparently had a chilling effect among foreign journalists there.

A sweeping political corruption investigation into high-ranking Chinese officials by reporters at Bloomberg was halted shortly before it was to be published, according to the *Columbia Journalism Review* in a 2014 report on the controversial story kill.[11] Critics say the news organization bowed to Chinese pressure. Shortly after the investigation was shelved, the reporting team fell apart.

Other troubles for journalists in China, include problems trying to access Tibet and covering ethnic conflicts in western regions of the country.

The *Times* reported in 2014 that dozens of reporters were "roughed up, detained, or shadowed by plainclothes police officers as they tried to work in far-flung provinces as well as the heart of the nation's capital."[12]

Although, some veterans who have been in the country for decades recall an environment that was much more oppressive to journalists years ago.

If you're a journalist who often covers controversial topics, or works with NGOs that some governments find troublesome, then you might want to even consider publishing under a pseudonym, according to Axelrod.

He says he's been turned down for visas by some countries—once immigration officials simply Googled his name.

But beyond just press freedom, you might also have limited access to common newsgathering tools, like the internet. CPJ also regularly releases its rankings of the world's most censored countries. Its list includes the usual suspects like China, Eritrea, North Korea, and Vietnam; but also Saudi Arabia, Cuba, and Ethiopia.[13] In these countries, access to information is restricted. Besides these countries' constant threats of arresting journalists—even at state-run media—the governments also heavily restrict mobile phone use access to the internet and satellite communication. They also muffle the voices of any opposition, and filter search engine results or block millions of websites, with expansive initiatives like China's "Great Firewall." These measures make it much more difficult to do your job.

But it doesn't mean that this censorship or these repressive policies against free speech make these countries any less of a news market. In fact, U.S. media are immensely interested in Iran, Cuba, and China. But your work as a journalist, especially as a freelancer, will be more difficult. If you are considering working in these countries as a freelance foreign correspondent, it might be wise to go only if you have a more formal and committed agreement with a well-known and powerful international news organization that can help you navigate the bureaucratic hurdles and journalistic challenges of reporting there.

Getting Around

As Szlanko notes, being able to tell stories regionally is important for a freelancer: "You have to think about whether it's an easy place to fly to and from," he says. Access to affordable transportation options can open doors to stories for freelancers in locations across the world. Without them, freelancers can be shut off from news and paychecks when stories are slow in their current home base.

For instance, most of Western Europe is well connected to other major cities. The same is true in most of the larger metropolitan areas of Southeast Asia. If a big story warrants your attention, you could easily travel to it outside your home base in a relative flash. Bus, rail, and low-cost flights are all plentiful in these regions.

Other parts of the world have less access to reliable and affordable transportation. Africa is one example.

These days, I think most freelancers agree that there are opportunities for storytelling in nearly every corner of Africa despite the limited presence by international media with the exception of major newspapers and broadcasters like the BBC and VOA, both of which have significant audiences in the continent.

The content from Africa ranges from the lasting consequences of the Arab Spring in countries such as Tunisia and Egypt (although North Africa is often included in the reign of hubs like London or Middle East bureaus), al-Shabaab terrorists in East Africa around Somalia and Kenya, Boko Haram terrorists in Nigeria, unrest and U.S. government drone bases and uranium interests in Niger, and power struggles throughout the governments across Africa.

Other recent notable stories include the intense coverage of the Oscar Pistorius trial in South Africa in 2014, the Ebola epidemic in Sierra Leone and Liberia, the 2010 World Cup in Johannesburg, and menacing pirates targeting commercial ships off the Horn of Africa—one confrontation of which inspired the movie *Captain Phillips* with the namesake hero played by Tom Hanks.

In the last 30 years, the main story themes from Africa have been the AIDS epidemic, deposed corrupt leaders and coups, famine, and genocide. Still extremely relevant stories today, they are often overshadowed by other current issues that have caught the attention of the restless searchlight.

So, there clearly is potential for freelancers to make a living working in Africa, especially since they face little competition from full-time staff counterparts.

The problem is the immense size of the continent—and the sporadic nature of news. It would be a challenge to solely report from just one country, Namibia, for example. The country offers some fantastic opportunities to report on wildlife, science, and ecosystems, and could be of interest to mainstream news organizations like National Geographic. But, that might not be enough to sustain you as a freelance journalist trying to cobble together enough work to fill days of reporting. So the challenge for Africa correspondents is being able to be mobile.

The continent is vast and aging transportation systems can be hard to navigate. If you're in Zimbabwe, and you're the "closest" correspondent to a breaking terrorist attack in a remote part of East

Africa, you'll face serious barriers in getting there quickly before the string moves onto someone else with better transportation access to East Africa.

As a freelancer, especially with new strings you're still coddling, you are often fronting the costs of your own transportation. Attempting to chase stories across such an expansive area can be cost prohibitive, especially for freelance foreign correspondents who are just beginning their career and professional relationships.

You're not just relying on flights to get you around Africa, but city taxis and even hired cars could take many hours navigating the challenges of driving through remote areas. It may not be as easy and convenient as other parts of the world that offer many low-cost flights, or safe, affordable, and direct rail travel from city to city.

However, if you're able to conquer this then you can make a career out Africa.

The landscape of regional and world access has changed elsewhere. That's affected how freelancers now choose their bases. One place that's changed for freelance foreign correspondents is Beirut. Lebanon has long been a hub for journalists charged with covering the whole Middle East, especially stories touching the Israeli–Palestinian conflict. But Szlanko complains that Lebanon has now been cut off from the Middle East. The war next door in Syria has isolated the country, and traveling to Israel can also be a hardship with travel restrictions to the Holy Land. In an increasingly competitive market, journalists are now looking to Istanbul as a base to cover the Middle East. It has two easy-to-access airports with a third one planned, and offers freelancers the freedom to cover the wars in Syria and Iraq, as well as Eastern Europe including Greece where the economy has collapsed and migrants are trying to make it to the EU.

Now, partly because of the city's access to the rest of the region, "there are tons of journalists in Istanbul," Szlanko says.

As you can see, the importance of regional access is a strong consideration for a location.

Happiness

Don't just view a reporting destination where you could spend months, if not years, living and work as solely an opportunity for a paycheck.

"That's a very important concern," says Szlanko. "Because if you are going to move to one of these countries you want to move to a place you will enjoy."

Choose somewhere that genuinely interests you. You have to be intellectually and emotionally invested in your new home. You must care about what's going on there—otherwise, your lack of empathy will be clear in your work. You must feel compassion for the people affected by the news there, or you'll quickly begin to disdain them and write with an easily identifiable bias. You truly will be a foreigner in a foreign land.

Andy Beale, a New Mexico-based journalist who spent two years freelancing in Ramallah, the political capital of the West Bank, was curious about seeing the Israeli–Palestinian conflict unfold from a different perspective. And what a world it was.

"It's a very different thing when you're living there," Beale says. Israel is just "12 kilometers away from Ramallah, but it takes you two hours to get there because of the checkpoint."

While many journalists based in Tel Aviv or Jerusalem cover the conflict, he was fascinated by witnessing the other side of the story: "I definitely got a picture of things from a different perspective than being based in Tel Aviv," he says.

Beale says, "Pick [a place] that interests you. I don't think it would be the best to pick something because you think there is work there."

And Beale is right. While going to a place just because there are work opportunities there might be financially prudent, it probably won't work out for you in the long run if you're not intellectually or emotionally invested in the country. You'll be bored. And avoiding boredom is the reason why you probably set out on this journey to a strange land anyway. Don't waste your time and money on work that doesn't interest you.

Beyond just intellectual satisfaction, however, whatever city, country, or region you choose must also appeal to you. Sure, the destination could stimulate professional interests, goals, and curiosities for a few weeks. But is it sustainable for the long term? Some of this comes down to how much you think you'll enjoy living in this place. There has to be something else besides the news that keeps you there. Hate the cuisine there? You probably won't last more than a month. Find the culture or society personally and deeply oppressive? It'll become more and more difficult to live there when you realize you're a guest, not a citizen. You have very few rights and no real mechanism to inspire change. You are just an observer.

Even simple things you take for granted at home like free parking, cheap clothes, and plentiful Wi-Fi can feel like luxuries when you have to adjust to a new life without them. Homesickness can quickly affect even the most hardened world travelers. And the yearning for the cultural conveniences of home can push you to tears. Simply read the personal blogs of the most compassionate, selfless people you can imagine, U.S. Peace Corps volunteers, to understand how the absence of familiar simplicities of life can affect your mood, perception, and affinity for a new foreign home.

Personally, I have a new appreciation for buying alcohol. I love how, in most of the U.S., I can simply walk into a liquor store (or even, in some cases, a pharmacy or grocery store) at almost any hour of the day and buy a cheap quality bottle of wine or whiskey and go about my day. The simplicity and freedom of this is pure joy, compared to living in countries such as Kuwait, Iran, or Saudi Arabia where alcohol is forbidden. Even in countries like Turkey and Australia, alcohol is so expensive lots of folks just stick to whatever the cheapest beer on tap is.

I also now value the long hours many shops keep in the U.S. Need an errand done on a Sunday evening in most of the world? You better wait until Monday. In the U.S., the land of 24-hour stores, convenience reigns.

Even doing laundry can be a pleasure when you realize how you've taken it for granted for so long. Just finding a laundromat in Moscow is like trying to track down a unicorn. I still haven't gotten an answer from a Russian on whether the concept of a laundromat is just so foreign that they don't exist there, or if some draconian Soviet-era regulation makes them an impossible business. You then have three options: hand wash your own clothes and hang them to dry (a horror in winter), borrow a friend's washer, or pay exorbitant prices at a hotel to get them cleaned.

Now, forget about the reality that washing machines are made of fairytales in many parts of the world; just having access to a dryer can be orgasmic. Even in the UK, Spain, and Australia, it's hard to find a dryer in most homes. That usually means laying out clothes on radiators to dry, draping them on dripping "clothes horses," or ironing the water out. Sure, dryers are huge, energy-hogging machines designed solely for the use of careless, lazy Americans, but they are a luxury to use when you no longer have access to them.

But often, it's not the absence of the tangible comforts of home, it's the cultural differences that may overwhelm you the most.

Working—and even living—as a female, LBGT person, or someone from a religious minority in a country with an oppressive government or conservative culture might also pose challenges to you.

Even veteran television foreign correspondent Martha Raddatz of ABC News has encountered overseas cultural hurdles in her work.

In 2008, she described her challenges as a woman in Saudi Arabia covering the announcement that the Bush administration intended to sell its Middle East ally 900 GPS-controlled bombs.[14]

While there covering the president's trip across the region, she decided to pop into the gym of the "American-owned Marriott" where she was staying. She says, the man at the reception told her, "Sorry, ma'am, but ladies are not allowed in here."

Understanding the common practice in Saudi Arabia of separating men and women, she offered a compromise: allow the women to work out after the men had had their chance.

She was met with resistance when the man at reception told her, "Sorry, ma'am, but that is not possible."

Even Raddatz's extensive experience in the Middle East still challenged her.

Gays might also face discrimination, especially in Africa. That's where Amnesty International reports 38 countries still outlaw homosexuality.[15] In Mauritania, Sudan, northern Nigeria, and southern Somalia, "Individuals found guilty of 'homosexuality' face the death penalty," according to the non-profit human rights group.

Obviously, you'll want to make reasonable personal accommodations to match the environment you're in if you believe you might be persecuted for your beliefs or lifestyle. If you're in Pakistan, don't go to a locals-only restaurant and demand ham. Don't dress like you're on a beach holiday when you're in especially religiously conservative neighborhoods. And don't act like a boorish drunk in countries where there are restrictions on alcohol. But overall, this is common sense. If you've gotten this far in your journey as a freelance foreign correspondent, you are already aware of the world's varying differences in attitudes about sex, gender, and religion.

If you think you might be targeted for what you are, try connecting with the local foreign correspondents' club. Their members should be able to tell you what challenges you might face, and how to avoid personal or professional confrontations. They should also be able to guide you to neighborhoods in the city that are the most accommodating to your lifestyle or beliefs. In sprawling Istanbul, for instance, micro-communities and neighborhoods run the entire spectrum from traditionally conservative to open and liberal. Choosing a community that will accommodate your personal beliefs or lifestyle without forcing you to hide in the shadows or worry about persecution will make your transition easier and more enjoyable.

Cultural differences aside, sometimes there's just the everyday quirks of a country that begin to grate on you. Take traffic. In Istanbul, traffic laws are often ignored. The madness on Turkish streets is enough to drive even the most mild-mannered motorists and pedestrians mad. To many Turkish drivers, traffic laws are mere suggestions. Watching a vehicle stop in rush-hour traffic before turning around on a one-way street is enough to send anyone over the edge. And just trying to safely cross the street in busy intersections means taking your life in your own hands.

In Myanmar, the common kissing sound people make at restaurants to call the waiters' attention might put you off.

Or the fleeting punctuality of friends, co-workers and interviews might begin to enrage you in countries where time is viewed with leisure and generosity.

In Russia, just navigating the country's social customs can be a challenge. Don't bring someone an even number of flowers—for those are meant for funerals.

But even the unpredictable cloudy, damp weather in London, or the relentlessly steamy summer in Singapore could be a shock to you.

Wherever you are, focus on taking the time and effort to ensure your own periodical well-being. Doing this could even help your productivity.

"Make sure you take care of yourself," Auger says. "When you make your own hours you may feel guilty if you aren't checking Twitter or reading the breaking news. But make sure you tune out and don't get too sucked into the news cycle. There are lots of interesting stories out there that you won't find sitting in your apartment on your computer."

No matter where you are outside your homeland, you'll be challenged. This is natural. It's part of living and working as an expat. It's part of the experience of exploring the unfamiliar. If you weren't challenged culturally, financially, socially, and physically, there'd be no reason to travel abroad. The best you can do is understand your destination's differences, and maybe even embrace them. The least these obstacles do is prepare you for the day when you might be called on to do some seriously challenging work personally and professionally: war correspondence. The daily struggles of just living, sleeping, working, eating, and surviving in a war zone make everything else you've done before just a bother—nothing more. We discuss the practicalities and safety considerations of reporting from war zones later in this book.

Calculus

Now comes the bubbling confluence of all of the factors you're weighing when choosing the ideal destination. Making sense of the countless considerations needed to wisely choose a destination is essential.

Simply put, "It is extremely important where freelancers base themselves," says Cengiz Yar, a freelance photographer who's hopscotched across news hotspots and faced the unique challenges that each presents.

Realistically, you won't find a spot that has everything you're looking for. But you'll have to weigh the news opportunities, competition, costs, regional access, and personal interests in your target destination against one another to come to a conclusion. Part of your decision will also have to come down to your trust in your gut, sense of adventure, and personal willingness to test your boundaries.

Szlanko ended up staying in Beirut as a base for his early freelancing efforts in the Middle East for just seven months. He felt there were other opportunities for him professionally and personally that existed elsewhere. He says he has no regrets, but suggests perhaps committing to a destination for about a year before deciding to move on. Giving yourself this amount of time will help you build a list of sources and contacts for stories, recruit new strings to cobble together a living, adjust to new living standards, and make personal relationships that will meaningfully attach you to your new home.

Selecting a destination is among the most important choices a new freelance foreign correspondent can make. It can mean the difference between early success and failure. But, no matter the outcome, you will learn from the experience. It will help you more thoughtfully select another location, improve your reporting skills, and quickly teach you the fundamentals of selling yourself and your work in the international media marketplace.

Putting It All Together

You may have always dreamed of living in a remote Tuscan villa with a sundrenched garden overlooking a sprawling vineyard. You might still imagine yourself telling the stories of the oppressed refugees who huddle into "temporary" U.N. camps. Your curiosity could be sparked every time you meet a Russian who adapted to a new life in post-Soviet times. But now, it's time to think about reality as a freelance foreign correspondent.

Your best strategy, as you consider a location, is to think positively but realistically.

"You should not over-romanticize things," says Fons Tunistra, who freelanced in Beijing just after Tiananmen Square.

Don't think every day will be filled with steamy Southeast Asian coups or rebellions against repressive African governments. Most of your day-to-day work, just like back home, will be filled with some drudgery and routine. But it will also include much more bureaucracy and paperwork.

And while your happiness and comfort at any destination you choose are paramount, you'll never be able to pay your bills with smiles and good thoughts. The challenge of choosing the right location for you is a very personal one. You'll have to evaluate all of the considerations that we've addressed in this chapter. You must balance your dreams with your realities. Unless you are independently wealthy and living off a trust fund, you'll need to find a way to make your dreams of living in a personally fulfilling location sustainable for the long term.

This means you might have to trade in your hopes of spending the late summer evenings picking herbs from your garden in the south of France for shooing away stray cats outside your Lagos walk-up. But don't worry; you won't be stuck there forever. Once you've developed a strong background as an international reporter with the contacts to match, it'll be easier to go somewhere else that might really live up to fantasies you've always had of sipping espresso in the Italian countryside in between high-intensity news cycles.

But now that you've come to your senses, it's time to get to work, looking for work.

Notes

1 *The Year of Living Dangerously*. Directed by Peter Weir. Performed by Mel Gibson, Sigourney Weaver, Linda Hunt. USA, Australia: MGM, 1982. Film.

2 *The Year of Living Dangerously*.

3 *The Year of Living Dangerously*.

4 "Bloomberg Opens New State-of-the-Art Office in Kuala Lumpur," *Bloomberg*, February 19, 2013, http://www.bloomberg.com/company/announcements/bloomberg-opens-new-state-of-the-art-office-in-kuala-lumpur/.

5 Zakaria, Fareed. "Whatever Happened to Obama's Pivot to Asia," *Washington Post*, April 16, 2015, http://www.washingtonpost.com/opinions/the-forgotten-pivot-to-asia/2015/04/16/529cc5b8-e477-11e4-905f-cc896d379a32_story.html.

6 Ariens, Chris. "Covering Patricia, Strongest Hurricane on Record, Won't Be Easy," TVNewser, October 23, 2015, http://www.adweek.com/tvnewser/covering-patricia-strongest-hurricane-on-record-wont-be-easy/275425. Accessed October 25, 2015.

7 *2014 Prison Census: 221 Journalists Jailed Worldwide*, Committee to Protect Journalists, December 1, 2014, https://cpj.org/imprisoned/2014.php.

8 "Challenges of Journalists Overseas becoming Worse," *Al Jazeera America*, May 26, 2015, http://tinyurl.com/q5crz45.

9 Landler, Mark and Sanger, David E. "China Pressures U.S. Journalists, Prompting Warning from Biden," *New York Times*, December 4, 2013, http://tinyurl.com/pwpultv.

10 Jacobs, Andrew. "Reporter for Reuters won't Receive China Visa," *New York Times*, November 9, 2013, http://tinyurl.com/ohvmkdl.

11 French, Howard W. "Bloomberg's Folly," *Columbia Journalism Review*, May/June 2014, http://www.cjr.org/feature/bloombergs_folly.php.

12 Jacobs, Andrew. "China Gets even Colder for Reporters," *New York Times*, December 17, 2014, http://tinyurl.com/qc6yya9.

13 "10 Most Censored Countries," *Committee to Protect Journalists*, 2015, https://cpj.org/2015/04/10-most-censored-countries.php/

14 Raddatz, Martha. "Reporter's Notebook: Second-Class in Saudi Arabia," *ABC News*, January 14, 2008, http://abcnews.go.com/Politics/story?id=4132767.

15 "Making Love a Crime: Criminalization of Same-Sex Conduct in Sub-Saharan Africa," *Amnesty International*, http://tinyurl.com/p34y7px.

3

COLD CALLING AND "THE VISIT"

You've made it quite far now on your journey to freelance foreign correspondence. You've zeroed in on why you are interested in this career path, what you're willing to give up to accomplish it, and where you want to go. Now, you must find out how to do it.

The last position you want to be in when you arrive in your target location abroad is to be jobless *and* hopeless.

Likely, you *will* be jobless. Not many news organizations are willing to gamble on an inexperienced journalist thousands of miles from home base to depend on when news happens. They might give you a try after you've arrived, but it's rare they will offer you a contract or other commitment prior to your arrival.

But it's being *hopeless* you must be more concerned about. When I mean hopeless, I don't mean you've arrived without a spark of ambition or dreams of success. I mean you've done no preparation prior to your departure from home to make arrangements with potential strings to which you can sell your work. You exist only to your friends and family at this location in which you plan to make your new home and career.

Your challenge: getting to the freelance hiring decision makers at hulking bureaucratic news organizations, gaining their trust, and convincing them to accept your pitches. There probably won't be any guarantee of payment or formal agreement between you and your potentials strings, before your arrival.

Don't expect this to be easy, either.

"Sometimes I think it can be very difficult to break through and find the right editor and for them to respond," says Zack Baddorf, a Brooklyn-based freelance foreign correspondent. But, "I understand from many editors perspective they are totally bombarded with freelancers."

Yet, the determined, persistent, and motivated will be best positioned to break through.

Likely, your initial contact with decision makers and potential strings will probably be only a casual heads-up that you'll be in a newsmaking destination and you're available to work. And, you'd like them to consider your story ideas. This is not much to go on for any guarantee for a career opportunity, but it's enough that, for many freelance journalists around the world, it's opened doors to success.

There are two main methods to accomplish this: either through your network or through "the Visit."

Networking

The web of international newsgathering organizations is complicated and intimidating. To an average person reading the *Tulsa World* newspaper, the story they see about an earthquake in Nepal might as well have been written by a *Tulsa World* reporter from their Nepal bureau.

LOL. By now you know better. There's no way the *Tulsa World* has a Nepal bureau, any international bureau, or even any international reporter. That Nepal story came from a news service like the AP or Reuters, their parent company BH Media, or like McClatchy or Tribune, or even another newspaper like the *New York Times* or *Washington Post*.

For the average TV news viewer, the source of a story could also be misleading. A story about the royal engagement at Buckingham Palace in the 6 o'clock news on a Miami station wasn't reported by one of its own reporters. Even if they signed off in the report with the station's call letters. Most likely, it came from an affiliate news service like CBS Newspath or FOX NewsEdge.

Trying to find the other actual news organizations that do real international newsgathering is frustrating. Yes, you can count the very big international news organizations: the *Wall Street Journal*, CNN, BBC, ABC, the *New York Times*, *The Telegraph*, VICE NEWS and BuzzFeed. But most news organizations even in large U.S. cities don't "do" foreign news. They might include it in their newspaper or TV broadcast, but they don't front the expenses or efforts to cover it on a regular basis. Those markets include Denver, Charlotte, Buffalo, San Diego, and Baltimore. Some markets like El Paso and Seattle may venture across the Mexican or Canadian borders—just because it's close and convenient. But they likely don't fly to their capitals of Ottawa or Mexico City to cover major legislation there or politics.

But, by connecting the dots, and finding as many real news organizations as you can that do international newsgathering, you increase your chances of finding someone who will accept your work.

This took me weeks. I used to think newspapers like the *Chicago Tribune* and the *Miami Herald* still had bureaus across the world. But now, they mostly rely on news agencies and their parent companies for foreign coverage. It's just one consequence of decades of cost cutting and declining readership. Sorting through where the news comes from is painstaking, and it's always changing. Not only do you have to find the places that cover foreign news, but eliminate the ones that don't pay.

Yes, that's right there are news organizations that expect you to work for free for them, to help them make more money. This is a common gripe among freelance writers. It a problem that is especially rampant in online media. News sites like the Huffington Post will often ask their vast network of contributors to provide them content, for nothing. Their hook? They give you "exposure."

My take: Screw exposure! Give. Me. Cash.

There are many freelance writers who *will* write for free, however—especially ones new to the game. But I do not believe you should ever work for free, unless you are doing it as part of efforts to volunteer your time and talent for a good cause.

One way to get a general ballpark idea of who doesn't pay, who does and by how much is to visit the site Whopays.scratchmag.com. The site allows freelance writers to anonymously post the rates of various news organizations and publications, and details how prompt they are with payment. Although many of these submissions are for U.S. online media that accept mainly essays from freelancers, it could give you a better idea of the few that might accept your work from abroad.

Your time is too valuable to do free work. Your investment of your time could better be spent convincing paying clients to take your work.

And don't just look at the big media to find paychecks. You don't need to do television stories every day for the BBC to make a living as a freelance foreign correspondent. Many lesser known news organizations cover foreign news, and can offer you a living. Bloomberg BNA's stable of publications like the

Daily Report for Executives, Daily Tax Report, and the *Daily Environment Report* have offered freelancers around the world reliable lifelines for decades. Their editors are professionals. They pay by the hour for your time. They cover your expenses, including travel to news-making conferences. And they pay promptly. Not to mention the fact that often the news you cover quickly becomes mainstream news, like international offshore tax havens.

Sure, the reporting can be a bit dry. Writing about the latest developments in EU accounting regulations can be both overwhelming for a non-accountant and monotonous. But it can be rewarding once you've finally grasped complicated issues that seasoned law and business professionals depend on your insight for.

It also helps you build your portfolio and your list of references. And it provides you a safety net while you pursue bigger projects for more mainstream media. This is why you need to cast your net as wide as possible, while looking for potential strings prior to your arrival. Trying to freelance just for Condé Nast is too risky. There is just too much competition—even if you're good. So, you need to gather together as many strings as possible to weave a safety net, while still pursuing whatever work you can initially convince the editors at Condé Nast to give you. Just don't focus solely on such big competitive name brand strings.

Now you have to find the decision makers. This is the hardest part of finding work.

Many of the folks who decide to hire freelancers are deep within the bowels of a news organization. They often have no profile on the news organization's website. And their contact information can be like trying to find the Loch Ness monster.

First, try to locate someone who can give you access to this gatekeeper personally, or who knows someone who can.

Do you remember that old professor who used to work for *USA TODAY* in the 90s? She might not know anyone who works there today, but she might keep in touch with an old editor friend who does knows someone working on the foreign desk. That's exactly who you need. You need a contact who can vouch for you, even as a third party, to the decision makers who hire freelancers.

It's time to start scouring your network. Look for old friends, colleagues, ex-girlfriends, office janitors—anyone who knows anyone at the news organizations that you want to work for

Nick Barnets had experience working in Manhattan media before he left for Athens to jumpstart his freelance journalism career there. He used that to leverage contacts and knowledge of the industry to help find strings like CBS Radio News that would accept pitches from him in Athens.

His advice though: "It's really important you get some experience in the industry and contacts before you start."

Before Maria Korolov went to Russia, she scoured her personal and professional networks looking for journalism job leads in the country: "I called everybody and anybody and asked whether they knew anybody in Russia," she says. "Networking is critical."

Even family connections can pay off.

John O'Dowd, who traveled with his girlfriend from his home in Ireland to find work in Canada, managed to eventually score a job as the lead producer of a popular radio broadcast in Vancouver through a family connection.

"Strangely enough my mother's friend back in Ireland, her nephew, was one of the head guys at Corus Entertainment," which owns the station he now works at, O'Dowd says. "I organized a meeting with him."

His introduction to this key decision maker, along with his producing talent, helped his risky adventure to Canada pay off.

"He was more than happy to give me a shot," he says. "Because he was originally from South Africa," and related to the same foreign challenges O'Dowd was experiencing as an Irish outsider in Canada.

Now, as a young recent journalism graduate, O'Dowd is leading a popular radio broadcast, instead of toiling away as a low-level script runner back home. When he does return to Europe, however, he'll arrive prepared with serious news skills under his belt.

Having someone prop open the office door to a decision maker—like a family member, friend or professional contact—gives you instant credibility. You're no longer some schmoe off the street who thinks he can write for the *Economist*. You're a verified journalist people have put their neck out on the line for.

But independent filmmaker and American University journalism professor Bill Gentile suggests a slightly different approach. Instead of casting a wide net to reach as many contacts as possible, he suggests narrowing down your approach.

"You have got to figure out what your talents are, and how you can apply them best to what's out there," Gentile says.

That means identifying what your strengths and interests are in journalism and targeting the media organizations that best align with them.

For instance, target media editors at news outlets that publish many stories on international conflicts, if you're interested in pursuing a career path in war correspondence. Don't waste your time on chasing down editors at purely feature publications.

While I believe you should be willing to write or report on any topic to give yourself the best chance at making a living, you should be methodical and persistent in locating the right contacts at however many news organizations you target.

So here comes the dreaded "cold calling" obligation. Pick up the phone and start calling people. But first, send them an email letting them know you are going to call or would like to set up a time to chat.

You need three things to do this: a name, a phone number, and an email address.

If I have no contacts at a news organization I'm targeting, I turn to Google.

Don't start Googling for the contact information for the head of CNN. It's useless. Even if you do get it, he doesn't have the time to even think about you. That's what his underlings are for.

Also, avoid targeting positions like the Vice President of Talent and Recruiting, because they deal mainly with finding seasoned journalists to hire full time in big positions that can take months to fill.

Instead, start searching for folks on Google with titles such as "Director of International Newsgathering," "Foreign Managing Editor," or "Supervising Producer of Foreign News." You'll then usually be directed to that person's Twitter, Facebook, or LinkedIn profiles, if there's no official bio for them. Social media are goldmines. If you get lucky, they will list their email address on these platforms. Most times, they won't.

So try to track down the people at that organization who already have put their company email addresses out there. You might be able to find the email address of the folks who put out press releases for the news organization, because they often list them at the top for reporters to contact.

Find a template. For instance, firstname.lastname@abc.com. Or flastname@abc.com. Sometimes you might just have to guess—especially if they have a hyphenated last name. Keep sending emails to different addresses until you hit the one that doesn't return an automated message indicating you've sent your message to an email address that doesn't exist in the system.

In your messages, write something brief like: "Hi, (name), I'm a reporter in (state, country, location), and I'm heading to (country) to freelance. I know you've got a busy schedule, but I figured you might be interested in some pitches from there, so I wanted to give you a heads up that I'll be available for you there starting (date). I'd love to chat if you have just a minute."

To your amazement, they will often respond, indicating they are interested or not. Sometimes, they will tell you that you have the wrong person and you should talk to someone else whose information they will provide to you. Repeat the email format to that person, but also mention their colleague so-and-so gave you their name to get in touch.

Sometimes, you won't get any response. You're a stranger. They are busy. They get things like this all the time—especially from people who aren't serious. But you are. So, follow up with a phone call.

Unfortunately, this type of "cold calling" can be terrifying for journalists.

"You do cold calling all the time on your day job," Korolov says. "But journalists have such a hard time doing it!"

Finding a number, picking up the phone, and making an out-of-the-blue call for most people, except telemarketers, is like singing on "American Idol" naked. It's shameful, intimidating, and keeps you up at night. Get over it.

There are only three scenarios that result: hooray, you reached the right person and you got their attention; you got the wrong number and person; or they hung up on you. None of this means you're a bad person or that you'll go to jail.

Most likely you've already experienced the worst of this in your daily work anyway. Most journalists have been hung up on literally countless times . . . and it usually takes a lot of pushing to get to that point anyway.

The most important part is just getting their phone number right.

If their office number doesn't easily turn up with their email address on Google, try searching their name and the area code of the city in which their news outlet is located. Usually their number will pop up in a press release or social media posting. Don't always count on the fact that your target contact will be at the headquarters of the news organization, however. They might be in the London bureau, Washington, D.C., or elsewhere. If you are interested in a particular region of the world, they might be based in the news outlet's closest hub, Singapore or Cairo, for example.

If that doesn't work, sometimes you might get lucky calling the main number. If it's an automated answering system, you may have the option to look for their name in the directory. Or, if an operator answers, confidently ask to be connected to the person you're looking for.

Give it a couple weeks after you first sent your email. Maybe send a short follow-up email. Then, call once you haven't heard back for a while, and follow the same format as your emails. What I did was create a spreadsheet tracking my progress in finding and connecting with freelance gatekeepers. I contacted many—about a 100. I listed the target contact's name, phone number, email, location, and the status of my last contact effort. On what date did I leave them a voice mail? Did they tell me to call back after their maternity leave? Did they tell me to get in touch with a colleague instead?

It's important you keep track of your progress, so you can weed out the news organizations that you aren't interested in, or the ones that aren't interested in you.

The Visit

Your end goal in contacting potential strings is to get the freelance hiring managers to agree to "the Visit."

Meeting a client in person really does a lot to open doors for you. They see that you are a real person. You're not crazy. You're not a risky maniac.

"I have found that meeting with people whenever possible is the best way to establish a relationship," Baddorf says.

The visit will show potential strings that it's clear you've carefully thought out your plan to work abroad, and you're not going to risk your weeks of preparation to torpedo your experience by churning out a poor product. It also shows you are dedicated to your plan. You're willing to front the time, effort, and expense of visiting them in person because you value your relationship with them.

Lots of folks underestimate the power of the visit. However, as you work as a freelancer, you'll quickly begin to learn and value relationships—often spending a significant chunk of your time nurturing them.

All you really need is a maximum of 10 minutes of the decision maker's time. Before I left for Istanbul, I cold called and met in person with editors from NBC News, CBS News, the *Washington Post*, Reuters, and others. It takes a bit of bravado to meet with these gatekeepers who are experienced, powerful journalists. To some, you are a nobody. To others, you are an opportunity.

But realize that you're simply earning their respect. Some relationships will work out, others won't. But the more people you meet, the more chances you have.

I'd recommend choosing two cities and consolidating the most visits you can during your time in those cities. For instance, a solid combination might be New York and London.

This doesn't have to be a huge burden to you. You only need a couple days in each location. And you don't need to stay in luxury. Crash with whatever friends you have in these cities. Or just stay in an Airbnb place or a hostel.

While in these cities, try to schedule your visits one after another, cramming in as many as you can while negotiating transportation between each. Ask if they'd like to grab a coffee. If it's in the afternoon, suggest lunch. Always offer to pay for them.

If they are short on time, just ask you stop by and simply hand them you're resumé or say "hi." If they've got a while, show them some of your clips or video work.

If you've been unlucky in getting in touch with the right decision maker at a target string, and you've got some spare time in your schedule, consider arranging a tour.

Perhaps you're visiting a large TV network, and you know that the tour will lead you through the heart of the network's newsroom. It'll take a bit of bravado, but you could always try dashing off to the nearest occupied desk of a news executive and throwing your resumé at them with a gleaming smile. Your tour guide certainly won't like it, but they won't be your boss anyway.

At the meetings that you've arranged come dressed professionally. As silly as it sounds, I once went to what I thought would be a "casual" drop-in to see a talent executive at ABC while I was visiting New York. I didn't expect the meeting to last more than a few minutes, and I had been suffering through blocks of walking through a Manhattan winter hellscape. I also didn't want to seem desperate by dressing up for a meeting that we both knew wouldn't last that long anyway. So, I decided to wear "dressy" jeans. The meeting was indeed short—and so was her interest in me, as she made a quip about my informal attire. Nothing ever came from that visit. It really is true that you only have one opportunity to make a first impression.

Sometimes you're short on time. Your first visit might be within just a half hour of your arrival in the city from a long plane, bus, or train ride. Your hair might have a few cowlicks from sleeping on windowsills or your suit might be wrinkled. To avoid looking disheveled if you don't have time to pop into the place you're staying in to freshen up, bring a small overnight bag packed with your dress attire.

Travel in your casual clothes, and once you've arrived at your destination, just duck into a bathroom for a quick change and brush.

Once you arrive at the front desk of where your meeting is planned, politely and charmingly ask the receptionist if you can leave your bag there. If she won't allow it (you know, bombs these days . . .) bring it with you and just explain to the potential editor you've just arrived in. Although, more than likely, an assistant will bring you up to their office and will invite you to leave your bag there.

Now, when you do finally sit down face to face with your potential editor or gatekeeper you want to maximize your limited time with them.

If you've never met or spoken to them in person, make sure you come across as confident, professional, and organized. Your most convincing effort, though, might be to try and find some kind of connection with them.

Hopefully, you've had a chance to do a bit of research on them before your arrival. Did you go to the same college as them? Do you know a mutual contact in the industry? Are you from the same town? Do you enjoy the same sports or root for the same teams?

All of these clues into their personal lives are often available if you do a bit of investigating on social media. But don't go overboard trying to make connections because you'll give away all the creeping you've done on them. Just try and make it seem organic, not like you've been plotting this meeting for weeks—which is actually what you really have been doing.

If you're still a stranger to them, you probably won't make a whole lot of progress in your relationship with them at this stage. So try to end your meeting with a promise to follow up with them when you are in-country when you will start sending them pitches.

If they've already showed some commitment to you and you know they've got a bit of time to spend talking with you, ask them some specifics about how to get started with them abroad.

What's the best way to file stories: FTP, email, Dropbox, or some other internal system? How many pitches would they like? An occasional one, or whatever you've got whenever you've got it? Do they want to be the first you call or email with a pitch? How should you get started with invoices? Do they require you to submit your invoices through an internal accounting system or will they take whatever you send them that you've drawn up on your own? How often do they pay? And, importantly, what do they pay? Is there anyone else you should meet: the unit's business manager, an assistant, a colleague who might also be interested in your work in another department? Do you need a company email address? Is there any way at this stage they could get you a company press card? Could they write a letter vouching for you during your visa or press accreditation process? Is there any equipment they provide their stringers? For instance, in Turkey, CBS sent me an audio recorder. Prior to that, I recorded audio with my iPod for my radio reports since I didn't have a proper audio recorder or microphone—which today I believe are still necessities in professional radio work.

Asking them specifics about your future role with them will prove to them you are serious and prepared.

Following your meeting with them *always* send them a prompt thank you note. Sometimes, I like to bring with me a few stamps and thank you cards to fill out and mail that day. But, if I suspect getting mail to them might be a bit slow or get lost in the shuffle, I may send them a sincere and grateful email.

Virtual Help

As a back-up to the foundation of contacts you've already laid for yourself, you should also seek out online communities relevant to your location and professional interests that could be a source for job leads.

Examples of this include Facebook groups like Global VJs. Full-time and freelance journalists from around the world are members of this group. Often, editors for organizations like the *New York*

Times or Al Jazeera will post urgent assignments for digital video producers and shooters for work abroad often in places like Egypt and Turkey. This is a great way to make a bit of money while also proving yourself to a potential regular string. Do great work and it could lead to a stable source of income through a professional relationship.

Regional Facebook journalism groups like the Moscow Hack Pack can also provide freelancers with work opportunities. More often though these groups function like online foreign correspondents' clubs where journalists connect colleagues to key newsmakers and provide helpful information when big stories breaks. But sometimes journalists will also ask for help locating fixers or inquiring for paid assistance on a story—especially if it involves translation work.

Ok, congratulations! You are nearly ready to board that one-way flight to the next chapter of your life. Exhausted already? Well, now it is *actually* time to get to work.

See you abroad.

PART II

On the Ground

4

REPORTING

To be a successful freelance journalist, you've gotta be a hustler. No matter where you are. Whether you're in New York or Sydney, freelancing as a journalist isn't a cakewalk. In fact, it's more like walking across hot coals. You're jumping from string to string, under intense pressure to make deadlines all before a short lull before the next intense spurt of work. This will be your life.

Mastering reporting abroad is not all that much different than reporting at home. You must develop sources, search for stories, pitch ideas, and then put it altogether in a compelling way. What makes it challenging is working with little direct supervision, often in a foreign language, and sometimes during periods of intense intervals of news and information.

Developing Sources and Finding News

Even before you land in your target country, you must work to find sources. These sources could be real humans who feed you story ideas or news tips, websites, newspapers, or even Twitter.

Just like finding potential strings, you must be meticulous and methodical in looking for sources of news, information and facts, and story ideas. Once again, you must begin this process prior to your departure from your home country.

Like any contractless independent worker—a web developer, electrician, artist—you are selling something. In this case, as a journalist, you're selling your talent as a storyteller and newsgatherer. But you're also doing much more than just reporting the news. You're selling news.

You see, your stories could light up the pages of a newspaper. Your words could dance off computer screens and iPhones. Your voice could slide into the imaginations of radio listeners and tickle their minds. But without news, you're useless. You're just a writer or photographer, not a reporter or photojournalist. You can't make a living just selling photos of cute kids eating ice cream cones in a hot Danish summer or writing about swans circling a quiet lake in London. You must find something that is actually happening and convince someone to pay you to tell the story of it. In the best case, you must be able to do this just about every day.

We've already talked about how the location in which you choose to base yourself directly affects the quality and quantity of news you can sell. Regardless, wherever you are, news isn't going to find *you*. You must do the legwork to find *it*—even if you're in a region that has a lot of news coming from it.

The first thing you need to do while still at home is to deeply understand what the issues are in the country you'll be moving to. Is there any ongoing migrant crisis there, war, political instability, or terrorism? In your preparation so far, you've probably already researched this.

Now, visit as many newspaper websites as possible. If you can already read the language, you'll be set up for more success. Otherwise, try and find the main English-language news site. You'll be surprised how common these are in cities across the world: from Phnom Penh and Moscow to Istanbul and Beirut. Also visit the sites of major television channels in the country. Even if you can't understand what they are saying in their news reports, you'll be able to get some kind of idea about the general themes of the stories.

Zack Baddorf, a Brooklyn-based freelance foreign correspondent, finds English-language newspapers in the countries he's visiting to be invaluable: "Whenever I can, when they have local English publications I will read them," he says.

Baddorf recalls while reporting from Ukraine he often depended on local publications for the most up-to-date information on the conflict there.

"That's where I'd get basically all my news on what's happening," Baddorf says. "I'd find out day by day, minute by minute from local publications."

To stay current on news, you should also maximize your use of social media to prepare for your trip abroad. First, create a daily Google alert with the name of the country you are targeting, and any major cities there and in the region. Each day you'll get an email summarizing the news with datelines or keywords matching your alert. These are invaluable, because they constantly troll news sites to give you a heads up on some key stories you might miss.

Next, turn to Twitter. Track down and follow the Twitter accounts of newsmakers like presidents and prime ministers, royal family members, key public figures, and political opposition leaders. Also, follow major local and foreign journalists, government agencies like police, fire, intelligence, counterterrorism, foreign and home offices, and academic institutions. Sometimes there will be specific lists of Twitter accounts like media and politics you can subscribe to. Otherwise, you should find the most powerful and influential journalists in the country and subscribe to the most relevant of the Twitter accounts they follow.

Do the same thing on Facebook and Instagram. Follow whatever people and organizations you think will be relevant to your work. Think broadly, too. For instance, don't ignore academic journals. If you're based in London, a significant medical or science story published by academics at Oxford could be an easy news story for you. Academics are always interested in getting publicity for their work. Also, "like" the pages of official bodies that regularly post press releases and updates like the United Nations and the World Anti-Doping Agency.

You should also consider subscribing to the RSS feeds of groups that regularly distribute news releases and media updates. One resource is Feedly. The website allows you to subscribe to a limitless number of RSS feeds from government offices, news organizations, etc., and constantly view the latest updates in a single location. It's a quick way to scan the most recent updates from primary sources each morning to generate story ideas and stay up to date on trends and issues. Best of all, these updates come direct from sources—so you can beat newspapers and broadcasters who might report on them the next day.

Finally, make a list of key contacts in your target country. This can be anyone from the spokesperson for your local embassy, to government press advisors and human rights activists. Reach out to all of them. Send them a brief email introducing yourself and the date of your arrival. Ask to be subscribed to any press email distribution list they have.

While you scour for contacts, try to find any foreign correspondents club in your target country. These days most of these physical clubs are just distant memories from the past. Like the very active

Istanbul Foreign Correspondents Club, most of the clubs today exist only virtually. Reach out to whoever makes the membership decisions and ask to be added. Despite their online-only presence, they can be helpful resources to find current information on key story contacts and ideas. Many journalists will also share their most recent professional newsgathering challenges and ways you can avoid repeating similar circumstances or mistakes. Be careful, though, with what you post in these electronic forums. In some countries, members suspect there are government or political moles embedded in these groups to track the activities of foreign journalists. You don't want to become a target, and you don't want to jeopardize your reporting.

In-Country

It's important that once you arrive in-country, you have a good grip on who the most important newsmakers are in your location and what people are talking about. That way you can dive right into work, without having to waste time trying to catch up.

O'Dowd recalls an embarrassing moment when he first started at his Vancouver radio station answering the call-in line as a new producer still unfamiliar with the city. Out of the blue, the city's well-known mayor called into the station and told O'Dowd his name: "I said 'And you are . . .?'".

Every new journalist to a country has similar stories, however. It can be tough trying to learn the dizzying number of key figures in a new city, not to mention the nooks and curvatures of the biggest issues, on which you could report.

"Just learning the geography of the place, learning all the political parties and what they stand for," can be a huge undertaking O'Dowd says. "It takes a long time."

Fortunately, once you've invested that time and reached out to news contacts you'll reach a point where the news will be easier to find, he says. Sources will start reaching out directly to you to share tips, other contacts, and story ideas.

To make it easier for you to connect with sources, visit a printing shop as soon as you can after you arrive in-country. There, you can get simple business cards designed and printed at a very reasonable cost. All you really need on the cards are your email address and cell phone number. Some freelancers also list the strings for which they most often report. You might want to consider asking the permission of each string you list before doing this, however, especially if you are a new freelancer for them or don't contribute on a regular basis.

When establishing relationships with sources, it's always important to get some facetime with them. If you know they might be valuable to your reporting, suggest grabbing a coffee with them or swinging by their office for a brief visit to introduce yourself. Leave the recorder and notebook back at home. These should be background-only meetings. You want this to be low pressure for them, and you want to allow them to speak freely. If, during your first meeting, they give you a story idea or a detail that seems interesting, politely ask if you can follow up on it with them. Never give a source the impression you're using them.

Think of it as beat reporting—not unfamiliar to any reporter who has covered a specific topic before like city hall, crime, or education. Learning the ins and outs of a beat and developing relationships with sources takes time but the effort can pay off.

You also want to recognize your limitations in foreign reporting, though.

You won't be able to beat the wires to news. Don't try. That is, don't work on getting the jump on news services like the AP or Reuters chasing barrel bombs in Syria, Yemeni rebel offensives, or typhoon fatalities in Taiwan. This sounds counter-intuitive right? You want to find original reporting that no one else has, right?

Consider this: many of the folks these news services hire to report locally around the world are, in fact, locals. They speak the language and they have decades-long relationships with government officials who can quickly give them information.

So, what you're doing when you try and compete with them is just tiring yourself out. And often, these kinds of "rocket attack" stories are routine and inconsequential to foreign media. Yes, your strings will report on them. But unless these stories involve the deaths of scores of people, most news organizations will run the wire reports but won't invest in commissioning a stringer because there's not much else to be told or it happens too often.

Instead, use the wires to supplement your own reporting. Instead of hopscotching across the Gaza Strip following mortar attacks, perhaps enterprise a story on *how* every single day citizens have been impacted by the attacks with information citing the latest wire reports.

Obviously, if you witness a huge story right in front of you, like the massive chemical explosion in Tianjin, China, in August 2015, you'll want to call your best string right away. While the wires will also report the explosion quickly, the story is big enough to share. Stories like these also provide many video opportunities that you can exploit.

Generally, however, you'll want to devote your time to the stories the wires miss, or to more encompassing stories that include information from several wire reports with your own original work.

It's also wise to constantly monitor local television news. Because you have already scoured the internet to watch local news broadcasts before your arrival, you'll have a general idea of what the biggest ongoing "talkers" are that TV stations are covering. Often local TV channels will beat international wires to big stories that could allow you to tip off your editors at home early, without you having to do much work at your end.

If you work in a major international city, local television networks will often have news-sharing partnerships with a broadcast string that you work for back home. For instance, CBS often shares content with UK news broadcaster Sky, and NBC airs reports from Australian broadcaster 7News. These international news-sharing agreements can be helpful to you, because you can often include material from these sources in your own work for your broadcast string back home. But certainly check with your editor first before you use any of this kind of content.

Keeping posted on the latest tabloids is also important. You'll rarely need to report follow-ups to what's going on in these newspapers because they mostly care about scandals and questionably sourced stories about celebrities. However, every now and then, they get an exclusive video of a high-profile figure or photos of a royal leader in a precarious situation leaked to them. If they are salacious enough, it can be worth pitching the idea to an editor at home and attributing the original story to the tabloid that first reported it. Obviously, though, check the track record of these newspapers. Just like back home, just because the *National Enquirer* has a story about a UFO abducting George Clooney overnight, doesn't mean it actually happened.

I am also a longtime supporter of "shoe leather" reporting. Get out on the streets and talk to everyday people. You've already put in the time to make inroads with officials and key public figures, now work on scouting out ways to tell your stories through real people.

The best example of this kind of reporting is any kind of refugee storytelling that has been humanized. Most stories on deteriorating humanitarian refugee situations throw in a few stats on the escalating number of people fleeing a war-torn region, the ballooning number of asylum seekers, along with reaction from some UN representative back in Geneva talking about how bad things have become. That's lousy reporting because it's not very compelling. The best stories are the ones that start with an emotional picture of a woman who's been widowed from the war, three of her four children are dead, and she's jobless and hopeless in a world that doesn't want her. There are plenty of opportunities to find people with the same stories, whether it's in Turkey or Thailand. Many reporters are just too lazy to go looking.

When you're out walking the streets of a city doing reporting also keep your eyes open to story ideas that might pop up anywhere unexpectedly. What changes are you noticing in society, the quality of living, or even the costs of everyday items?

Examples of these enterprising kinds of story are especially easy to find in countries like Russia. Big stories like the collapse of the ruble and the country's slowing economy can easily be told on a micro level through the rising cost of things like rice and meat pies. Pop into a few small shops run by struggling owners, and you've got yourself a pretty good story illustrating the new daily challenges of living in Putin's Russia.

An excellent example of an enterprised featured story is the following Associated Press piece on the emerging tug-of-war influences between development and religion at one of the world's holiest cities: Mecca.

"Saudi Overhaul Reshapes Islam's Holiest City Mecca"
Associated Press® (p)(c) 2014. Used with permission. All rights reserved.
By Aya Batrawy
October 1, 2014

MECCA, Saudi Arabia (AP)—As a child, Osama al-Bar would walk from his home past Islam's holiest site, the Kaaba, to the market of spice and fabric merchants where his father owned a store. At that time, Mecca was so small, pilgrims could sit at the cube-shaped Kaaba and look out at the serene desert mountains where the Prophet Muhammad once walked.

Now the market and the homes are gone. Monumental luxury hotel towers crowd around the Grand Mosque where the Kaaba is located, dwarfing it. Steep rocky hills overlooking the mosque have been leveled and are now covered with cranes building more towers in row after row.

"My father and all the people who lived in Mecca wouldn't recognize it," said al-Bar, who is now Mecca's mayor.

As Muslims from around the world stream into Mecca for the annual hajj pilgrimage this week, they come to a city undergoing the biggest transformation in its history.

Decades ago, this was a low-built city of centuries-old neighborhoods. Over the years, it saw piecemeal renewal projects. But in the mid-2000s, the kingdom launched its most ambitious overhaul ever with a series of mega-projects that, though incomplete, have already reshaped Mecca.

Old neighborhoods have been erased for hotel towers and malls built right up to the edge of the Grand Mosque. Historic sites significant for Islam have been demolished. Next to the Kaaba soars the world's third tallest skyscraper, topped by a gigantic clock, which is splashed with colored lights at night.

"It's not Mecca. It's Mecca-hattan. This tower and the lights in it are like Vegas," said Sami Angawi, an architect who spent his life studying hajj and is one of the most outspoken critics of the changes. "The truth of the history of Mecca is wiped out . . . with bulldozers and dynamite. Is this development?"

Critics complain the result is stripping the holy city of its spirituality. They also say it is robbing the hajj of its more than 1,400-year-old message that all Muslims, rich or poor, are equal before

God as they perform the rites meant to cleanse them of sin, starting and ending by circling the Kaaba seven times.

Mecca is revered by hundreds of millions of Muslims worldwide. They face the Kaaba every day in their prayers. The Grand Mosque is one of the few places in the world where Muslims of all stripes gather—Sunnis and Shiites, secular Muslims, mystics and hard-liners.

Overseeing Mecca is also a key source of prestige for Saudi Arabia's monarchy. The past two kings—the current one, Abdullah, and his predecessor, Fahd—have adopted the further title of "custodian of the two holy mosques" to boost their status, referring to Mecca's Grand Mosque and Muhammad's mosque in nearby Medina.

Now Mecca is being molded to a particularly Saudi vision that bolsters the rule of the Al Saud royal family.

Two forces shape that vision. One is raw, petrodollar-fueled capitalism. Mecca's planners are largely catering to wealthier pilgrims by focusing on construction of five-star hotels, surrounding the Kaaba in marble-sheathed luxury. Nearby, pilgrims can shop at international chains, including a Paris Hilton store and a gender-segregated Starbucks.

The other force is Wahhabism, the strict, puritanical interpretation of Islam that the Al Saud rulers elevated to the country's official doctrine. Saudi kings, for example, have given Wahhabi clerics a monopoly over preaching at the Grand Mosque. In return, the clerics staunchly back the monarchy.

One tenet of Wahhabism is that Muslim tombs or sites connected to revered figures—even the Prophet Muhammad, his family and companions—should be destroyed to avoid veneration of anything other than God. It's the same iconoclastic zeal that has prompted militants from the Islamic State group to blow up Muslim shrines in Iraq and Syria.

In Mecca, hardly any site associated with Muhammad remains. Many were destroyed in previous expansions of the Grand Mosque in the 1980s and 1990s, and the new development is finishing off much of what remains. In 2008, for example, the house of Abu Bakr, Muhammad's successor as leader of the Muslim community, was razed to make way for a Hilton.

The country's top religious official, Grand Mufti Abdul-Aziz Al-Sheik, backed such demolitions last year, saying "the removal of such things within the expansion is necessary."

The urban renewal is necessary, Saudi officials say, to accommodate hajj pilgrims whose numbers are expected to swell from around 3 million currently to nearly 7 million by 2040.

The $60-billion Grand Mosque expansion will almost double the area for pilgrims to pray at the Kaaba. Around half the cost went to buying about 5,800 homes that had to be razed for the expansion, said al-Bar, the Mecca mayor. Domes and pillars dating back to rule by the Ottoman Empire are being pulled down to put up modern facilities.

Another mega-project is Jabal Omar, a hill on the mosque's west side. The hill—a landmark in the city—was levelled and in its place, construction of around 40 towers is underway, mostly for luxury hotels providing some 11,000 rooms. The first of the Jabal Omar hotels, a Hilton Suites and the Anjum Hotel, just opened in the past few months.

On the mosque's south side stands the 1,972-foot (600-meter) clock-tower skyscraper, part of a completed seven-tower complex that was built after tearing down an Ottoman fort on the site.

Also underway is the Jabal Sharashif project, in which a slum that largely houses Burmese and African migrants is to be torn down to build a new neighborhood for Saudis, along with hotels. A four-line metro system is planned for the city, along with a high-speed rail line to the port city of Jiddah, where the area's airport is located, and to Medina.

The Grand Mosque's expansion is being headed by the Saudi Binladin Group, which also built the clock tower. The Binladin family has been close to Al Sauds for decades and runs major building projects around the country. Al-Qaeda's late leader Osama bin Laden was a renegade son disowned by the family in the 1990s.

Speaking at a public forum in Jiddah in May, Nawaf Binladin, whose father is chairman of the conglomerate, said people are constantly asking if all this construction is needed.

"This can be answered in one moment in this image," he said, flashing a picture of tens of thousands of worshippers praying in the street because there was not enough room inside the Grand Mosque.

But many in the audience were not convinced. Saeed al-Ghamdi, a former Saudi diplomat, said he thinks greed is the main motivator.

Muslims around the world have an "intimate bond" with Mecca, he said. "It is not a place for one businessman or one company."

Mecca's planners didn't have to build so close to the Kaaba, overwhelming the around 13-meter-high (13-yard-high) structure, said Irfan al-Alawi, a Saudi who heads the London-based Islamic Heritage Research Foundation. The hotels could have been built miles away and transportation improved.

"Already we are losing the spirituality," he said. Pilgrims admire the clock tower instead of "looking at the Kaaba and admiring the house of God."

Essam Kalthoum, managing director of the government-owned Bawabat Makkah Company, which is involved in a number of projects around the city, acknowledged that "it would be a farce" to say financial motivations are not coming into play.

But he said the main goal is to increase space for pilgrims.

Kalthoum showed a gift from a Turkish foundation he had just received: a photo of Mecca from the late 1800s.

"This is painful," he said. "For those of us who witnessed some of this, it brings back memories."

But he pointed to the Kaaba in the photograph. "Because of this place," he said, "the old markets and buildings had to go."

I think this is a good illustration of a unique foreign-datelined story for several reasons.

First, the writer found a unique take on Mecca. This holy city has been written about for centuries. It's a focal point of Islam and of the Middle East. Yet, at no other time in its history is Mecca facing such a tide of change from one of the very things it's supposed to separate Muslims from during their visit: the allure of divisive commercialism. This is a holy site where spiritual equality is paramount, yet the dimensions of the very place at the center of it are unequal: new vs. old, traditional vs. modern.

One quote in the story especially illustrates this struggle from architect Sami Angawai: "It's not Mecca. It's Mecca-hattan. This tower and the lights in it are like Vegas."

Yet, it's also characters like Angawai who the writer relies on to move the story forward. Not only does the reporter find a unique angle to the modern-day challenges facing this ancient city, but she tells it through the prism of the people on the ground, not the high-ranking clerics or bureaucrats. The journalist draws readers in by painting a picture of a sweeping, Middle Eastern landscape being built before their eyes.

Finally, the reporter finds an issue that foreshadows something larger. The story isn't just about the relentless growth of Mecca and the unstoppable greed some believe it now embodies, but the price it will soon pay. In fact, nearly a year after this story was published the toll of Mecca's growth turned deadly. A construction crane collapsed through the roof of the Grand Mosque, killing more than 100 people.

Then just days later a stampede during the start of hajj killed some 1,400 people. Hundreds more were injured. It was the worst tragedy there in 25 years. Reports blame crowds of confused anxious pilgrims rushing to complete religious rituals in a hot, chaotic area and a slow rescue response for the high death toll in the mayhem.

The AP story helps illustrate the breaking points in Mecca between the unstoppable wave of Muslims who seek religious fulfillment clashing with the poor management of the pilgrimage amid Mecca's relentless pace of development.

Remember, you're abroad for a reason. Don't just include a few lines from a press release and ring up a government contact for reaction. Like the AP story from Mecca, you should strive to include as much color and local insight as you can to bolster your storytelling. Experiment with new ways to tell stories, especially if you've got the space to do so. Try explaining larger issues through characters, spray your story with on-the-ground color and imagery, and find symbols that stand for something bigger like religious strife or economic turmoil.

Pitching

Pitching is a skill best honed through practice.

If you're new to pitching story ideas—maybe you're a sports writer who covers the local high school beat at home without many opportunities to enterprise news—start learning how to sell stories now. Finding stories is the first step to financial success in foreign news.

"If you can identify a good story, then the writing becomes much clearer, the reporting becomes much clearer and you'll have the interest of editors who will have a stake in it," says Robert Steiner, an accomplished journalist who teaches at University of Toronto's Munk School of Global Affairs.

"You have to find your own stories, and you have to know why most of your story ideas won't work," he says.

The best pitches are tailored to their audience. I'm not necessarily talking about the kinds of viewer, listener, or reader who might be interested in your story, but what the commissioning editor or producer is looking for, the news organization's style, and its content themes.

"There is a lot of difference in how I pitch my stories for each string," according to Baddorf. "Some outlets are interested in profiles, some are interested in hard news, some are interested in a specific kind of journalism like conflicts."

Here is an example. My pitch to NPR for a story on what Australia is doing to improve the Great Barrier Reef will be different than my pitch to CBS Radio News. Both are radio—but both tell stories very differently. NPR will want my pitch to be detailed: why is this important, where can I get good sound to tell the story in a compelling way, and how many sides can I get to talk? I'll have several minutes to tell the story. For CBS Radio News, by way of contrast, my pitch needs to be much more succinct. How can I get a busy mom in Kansas City driving into work at 7 a.m. on a Wednesday to care what's happening on another continent? The Kansas City mom might only listen to CBS Radio News briefly once a day. The average NPR listener might spend hours listening on a weekend. And CBS needs me to tell a compelling story in a challenging 35 seconds. So both have different requirements for pitches, based on their styles and listeners.

It's important you gather some intel on to whom to pitch, what to include, and how often, with your strings. You don't want to send too many pitches—like several a day, if your string appears not to be that responsive or has told you they don't have the budget to commission all of your stories. Instead, work on crafting the stories you do pitch.

"You have to walk a fine line between being respectful to the time it takes for an editor to make a decision and the urgency of your story idea," says freelance foreign correspondent Josh Baker.

Like Baker says, getting an editor interested in your pitches can be a challenging balancing act. You want to grab their attention, yet many times they can take days or even weeks to respond to your query.

In any other line of work, it would be unprofessional to not respond promptly to emails or calls, but perversely in journalism—a profession dictated by time and deadlines—it's standard, Steiner says. Unfortunately, this is something you must learn to cope with. But there are measures you can take to get editors to be more responsive to you.

The best way to pinpoint the reporting needs of a string is by building relationships with key editors there—something you've hopefully already started while preparing at home.

"More often than not the key to getting commissioned or a contract is around your ability to build a relationship with those you are pitching to," Baker says. "It's much easier to pitch to a friend who is stressed, than a stranger who is stressed and doesn't really care."

Also, look at the stories the strings you're working with have already done from freelancers.

For instance, one wire service told me while I was working in Australia that they didn't usually accept enterprise pitches from freelancers. The editor said most of the longer feature stories were reserved for full-time correspondents. Instead, they relied on freelancers to fill in the news holes with general assignment work.

And get used to rejection. Not every story you pitch will survive. To combat failure, do what writer Beth Winegarner suggests in a story for the non-profit U.S. journalism organization Poynter, "Pitch more than you can write."[1] But, deliver on everything you pitch.

Reporting

The meat and potatoes of your work is, of course, your reporting. However, there are a few differences from your work at home.

First, you should always be skeptical of all information. Don't cite anything in your own reporting without attributing it. This is journalism 101, but even more important when you're in countries that have a press that is still developing.

On several occasions in Turkey, the local newspaper attributed wrong information to the wrong people. Using this information in your own reporting, no matter how many outlets in your country are reporting it, jeopardizes your own credibility if it's wrong. Otherwise, you generally want to confirm all your information with a reliable source—sometimes two.

If you can't verify the information yourself, but it's big enough like the death of a president, make sure you attribute the news organizations reporting it. If it's from an official government-owned or -operated news organization, simply attribute the information with "according to state media."

Although I've come across many instances of flat-out wrong—even fabricated—reporting in several parts of the world, I can't determine whether the journalists behind the reporting have nefarious intentions, are sloppy, or are just working with lower standards than journalists in most Western countries.

My guess is in many countries the journalism we're used to—factual, timely, objective reporting—is too new to fully value or embrace. I believe this is the case in Russia where for decades under Communist rule, all media were controlled and censored. And, in many cases you could argue Putin's Russia still has a hand in the media today. Ultimately, though, Russia has only had "free" media for about 25 years since the fall of the Soviet Union. Whereas the U.S. has had a free press for centuries. Therefore, in some countries with developing democracies, journalists and the public simply aren't exposed to high-caliber reporting regularly enough to place a premium on it.

The other difference between reporting at home and abroad is your access to public information. Countries like the U.S. and UK have extensive freedom of information acts which provide provisions for members of the public, including journalists, to request specific information and documents from the government. But those laws don't exist in many other countries. And even if they do, they can require intimidating and time-consuming processes that might not even be worth your effort.

Sometimes trying to get any information at all can put you at odds with the country you're in.

After the massive August 2015 chemical explosion in Tianjin, China, several foreign journalists were confronted by police while trying to report from the scene of the deadly blast. At one point, CBS News foreign correspondent Seth Doane was accosted by police while shooting video outside a hospital.[2] He was escorted away by authorities that tried to block his crew from filming.

Examples of this extreme kind of treatment by the government with the press is harder to find in places like the U.S. where freedom of the press is a prized right.

In some countries, navigating unique libel laws can be a challenge.

Freelance foreign correspondent American Patrick St. Michel was confronted by Japan's differing privacy and press laws when he began reporting there: "In general, you can still be sued successfully even if you are reporting the truth about someone else, or a company," he says. "If it hurts that person's reputation, they can win a lawsuit—even if everything is correctly reported. This is a big determent for sources to talk to reporters—and for reporters and publications to publish more investigative pieces."

Time will also affect your reporting. The differences in time zones from your international location and your editors around the world will impact everything from when and how you pitch, to when you do actual newsgathering. For example, while it might be Monday afternoon in Australia, it could still be overnight on Sunday in New York. If you have a critical need to travel for a story, and your editor doesn't come in for hours, you'll be stuck waiting to get approval for the expense while your transportation arrangements are put under the wire. If you need elements or quotes from a source back in the U.S.—say a State Department spokesman—for a story you're working on half-way across the world, you'll have to wait until that person gets in the office in Washington, D.C., before you can finish your report.

When you are reporting, try to forecast what elements you'll need to complete your story, and which ones you anticipate will be impacted by time zone differences. Get started on those first. Remember, this will also impact your deadline. If your deadline is by close-of-business (5 p.m.) in the U.S. on a Tuesday, you'll have to finish your story by 6 a.m. Wednesday if you're working in Tokyo. Chances are you're not going to pull an all-nighter. So realistically, you'll want to finish your story by Tuesday night in Japan, which will be Monday morning in the U.S. So, be sure to keep track of time differences if you have elements you're gathering across the world.

Time zones will also be a problem when strings want to reach you. I can't tell you how many times I've answered my phone while inside a club or five drinks into my night with friends. While it might be midday in London, it's Happy Hour in Singapore. If it's a routine non-urgent phone call, savvy editors will know what time it is at your destination and will wait to call you at a better time, or simply reach out by email. But, occasionally a naive network desk assistant will phone you, unaware of the string of incomprehensible slurred words you're about to shout at them over the wails and hollers going on at your weekly trivia night.

And since your work covers so many different time zones, it's impossible to always work in an "office" as a foreign correspondent, and to keep office-like hours. Your "9 to 5" is often split up into bursts of activity.

Your schedule might look like this:

7 a.m.	Wake up and check your email. Spend the next couple hours immediately filing on a story that broke overnight
9 a.m.	Get breakfast, get dressed, go to the bank to deposit a check, then walk to the grocery store to do some food shopping
12 p.m.	Make lunch
1 p.m.	Your editors are in their offices back in the U.S. You get back to work pitching them stories
2 p.m.	You get offered an assignment, or you follow up to the story you filed on right after you woke up. You spend the next three hours frantically trying to gather elements for your stories before everyone leaves their offices at the end of their workdays where you're based
5 p.m.	You start writing your story for the day
7 p.m.	You file your story and do some prep work for ideas you want to pitch to your editors the next day. You also check the progress of the other stories you've been working on that weren't day-of news that demanded your attention right away today
8 p.m.	You cook dinner, or head out with friends to do a little socializing
11 p.m.	You come home and you go to bed

This is a strange work schedule, right? Your workday is broken up into chunks, as you try to straddle the time zones at your destination and at your strings' editors' office locations around the world.

Your schedule will also often be affected by holidays, both at home and abroad. You'll have to adjust your reporting and pitching timing to account for not only Christmas, Easter, etc., but for the Thai New Year and Buddhist holidays if you're in Bangkok. That's why it's also wise to have a few evergreen stories you can work on when things are slow on holidays.

These varying schedules and work times will certainly challenge you.

For example, one of your radio strings might call you at 3 p.m. your time, asking if they could record a couple "debriefs" of you over the phone talking about a story that just broke in your country. Often, despite them calling during normal "business hours," you are not in the office. Rather, you're walking down the aisles of the grocery story concentrating on which kind of cheese you want to purchase. You probably have no idea what story the caller is referring to, and you definitely don't have enough information to talk about it that would make any sense. How could you? Sometimes you can't know what's happening *all* the time. At the moment, you're focusing on the minutiae of living abroad and having a life. So if you get a call like this, simply ask for the caller to email you the story to which he is referring and tell him you will call right back. If he does want you to confirm details of the story, you'll need to stop what you're doing and get started making some calls and sending emails to verify elements of the report that was sent you. If he simply wants your reaction or analysis of the story, take a moment to review what was sent, an additional minute to check a few other sources, and call back to do the debrief he requested.

Don't try and bluff a report to a string. Even if they are calling you about a breaking news report that the prime minister of the country you're in is resigning, still take a moment to gather together some facts. Don't try and talk in circles about how the embattled prime minister was under investigation for corruption and how he was widely disliked by voters. Because they'll probably ask you to describe what he said in his statement in announcing his resignation, what happens next, and how the rest of the government is reacting to the news. As a result, your string will catch you in your lie trying to fake that you know what you're talking about. It will make you appear unprofessional. Simply be honest, tell them you're out doing some grocery shopping, and you'll call them right back to get up to speed for them on what they are requesting. Usually, they'll understand.

If I'm covering a days' long big story that I know will involve frequent updates, like the G20, then I'll try to prepare myself for being ready to respond to strings at a moment's notice: whether it's 6 p.m. or 6 a.m. That means I'll stay away from pubs, and any activities that could distract me from my work for a prolonged period of time: like retiling my bathroom. What a good excuse to avoid housework, anyway!

However, in some cases you can make time zones work to your advantage. They are especially helpful when working on story pitches. If you're in Istanbul and want to pitch a good story to an editor that'll be ready for them first thing Monday morning when they get into the office, you have virtually all day to work on doing the groundwork for it. Essentially, you have until 4 p.m. Istanbul time if you want to send your editor your pitch by 9 a.m. New York time.

While getting the nuts and bolts of stories is similar to reporting at home, you'll be confronted with new challenges. How you're able to navigate around them will test your resolve as a true foreign correspondent.

Tracking Your Progress

When you're working for several strings at once, keeping track of all your deadlines and stories can be a dizzying prospect. There are many steps to reporting just a single story: probing its viability, putting together a pitch, selling it, interviewing and writing, publishing or airing, and collecting payment. If all this work only nets you, say, $200 for the story, then you must work on several at once to make a living and have a regular stream of income.

Once again, to sort through all this, I like to make a spreadsheet tracker.

For work on stories that stretch over several days, I will first slug my story on a line in the spreadsheet and write a few words describing what I think the story is about.

For instance, "the rise in beard transplants in Turkey."

Usually, something I see on the street, in a newspaper, or from an actual human source will spark my interest in a story idea. But they're not always easily doable. So determining a story's viability is essential. It's always embarrassing when you pitch a story an editor loves and wants it with a quick turnaround, but you don't have enough elements already together to pull it off and meet deadline. Sometimes this can end relationships with strings. I always like to have some kind of idea whether a story can be done, and if so, how long it will take, so I can discuss it with the editor when they accept my pitch.

"For a pitch to work you need a good idea, your facts inline and it needs to be viable," Baker says.

At a bare minimum you need two things to pull off a story: facts and interviews. If I'm working on a story about the explosion in the number of men seeking fuller beards by getting doctors to implant hair into their face, then I need to talk to a few medical clinics that perform the procedure and find out how many more procedures they've done this year compared to previous years. If there is an association of dermatologists or hair transplant specialists, then I'll also need to check with them to inquire about whether they keep yearly statistics on the procedures.

But, I also need a doctor to agree to an interview. And, challengingly, I also need to find a man who was ashamed of his thin beard and got the embarrassing procedure done, who's willing to speak to me on the record. It's even more difficult if I need that embarrassed beard transplant patient to agree to speak to me for radio or TV interviews.

Usually, I'll probe around to see whether it's possible to arrange any of this before pitching. If I pitch the beard story, and no doctor wants to share with me the contact information of any of their patients for privacy reasons, and I can't find anyone through third-party sources like Facebook, I'm screwed.

Determining a story's viability can be time consuming, especially if it's difficult to get, such as finding a survivor of rape in a refugee camp to talk to you or an Iranian intelligence official to reveal the country's nuclear activities. Many freelancers will complain how much time this takes up—especially if they can't find any editors interested in it. You've just done a lot of groundwork for a story for nothing. However, I just don't see any other way around this. Pitching several stories to a string that you can't do is a certain way to torch your relationship with them. This is why you should always have stories developing at varying stages.

Once I've determined a story's viability, I'll pitch it to the string I think the story might be most appropriate for or the editor who might be most interested in it. I'll include the date I called or emailed the pitch in the spreadsheet line. If they don't respond in a few days, sometimes I'll follow up to hear their thoughts on the idea once more.

If they accept the pitch, I'll get started on reporting it. All the groundwork I've already done helps knock out the story quickly, and also allows me more time to gather any multimedia elements I need like photographs.

Once I finish the story I will send it. When they reply that they've accepted it, I'll send the invoice and log the date, before entering when I received payment. Sometimes editors will require changes or ask I gather additional elements. So I will usually wait until they are satisfied with the story as is, before actually sending them the invoice.

Obviously, more complicated stories take longer; easier ones can be done in just a few hours. Even if a story takes just an hour of my time, I always keep track of when I filed it for air or publication and when I received payment. That way, if it's been several weeks (or months) without being paid for a story, I can go back and examine my records.

Often as a freelancer you'll be managing multiple projects, so whatever way you find helps you to best manage your time and story progress will help you and your bank account.

Notes

1 Winegarner, Beth. "6 Tips for Getting Gigs as a Freelance Journalist," Poynter, October 2, 2012, http://www.poynter.org/how-tos/advice/190234/6-tips-for-getting-gigs-as-a-freelance-journalist/. Accessed September 27, 2015.
2 Mullin, Benjamin. "Journalists Covering Tianjin Explosion meet with Interference," Poynter, August 14, 2015, http://www.poynter.org/news/mediawire/366315/journalists-covering-tianjin-explosion-meet-with-interference/.

5

MANAGING MONEY

The elephant in the room for many freelance journalists is making money and getting paid. If you're new to the world of freelancing, get ready for a big financial wake-up call.

"As a freelancer there is undoubtedly added pressure, not only do you have to do the work as you would in a staff job, but you also have to generate new work at the same time," freelance foreign correspondent Josh Baker says.

Former freelance foreign correspondent Daniel Bach laments that making a living as an independent journalist is a challenge: "Right now, in the era of journalism we're in it can be hard to stay busy and to find people that are buying."

Before we embark on navigating the world of freelance finances, let's get something out of the way: you will not get rich. In fact, the best you'll probably do is *survive*. Any idea you have about foreign correspondents lounging poolside in gated Hiltons while on assignment, attending evening balls and dancing with diplomats is ludicrous. This might be the lifestyle of a handful of full-time foreign correspondents with the expense accounts of major news organizations, but the global recession has just about done away with almost all of this. Your reality? Living in a crowded apartment and sleeping in hostels or airport benches while on assignment, attending press conferences where the only luxury in sight is free lukewarm coffee, and dancing in the dark because you can't afford electricity.

This is true with nearly every freelance foreign correspondent I have talked to. Even the ones who have a monopoly on certain strings in their country and regularly work aren't necessarily doing better financially than they would with their same reporting skills working back at home. To do this, you must do it for the experience, not the money.

Like Baker, most freelance foreign correspondents ride the valleys of lean times and the peaks of fat paychecks because their reward is not financial but experiential. Reporting abroad adds zest to life and variety to work. This is no "9 to 5" office job, and most freelancers wouldn't want it any other way.

"You are going to work more than 10 hours a day, 6 or 7 days a week, [which will have] a big impact on your work life balance," Baker says. But, "I love this diversity and for the most part, the pressure. It really keeps life interesting."

Therefore, you must define your own "success."

For me, my goal when I first became a freelance foreign correspondent was to sell one foreign-datelined story. That's it. If this career experiment I risked so much on went sour, I at least would have one story I could point to for some shred of success. And when I did sell that first story, I felt completed, accomplished, and hungry for more.

Soon after, my definition of success changed. I then wanted to find work with more high-profile strings. When CBS Radio News, and later NPR's "Morning Edition", aired my reports I felt like my experiment was finally starting to produce serious satisfaction for me.

When I began regularly finding enough work to make my experiment sustainable for me, I began thinking about the long term. That's when my goals transformed into something financially focused.

I started making weekly financial goals. I aimed to make a certain amount each week. To meet that goal I had to focus on finding, developing, and pitching the best stories, and maximizing their financial yields.

Ultimately, this approach didn't earn me much money. But it did earn me the freedom to live somewhat comfortably at my international locations, while pursing the foreign journalism that most interested me. In essence, that was the original goal I first wanted when I boarded that plane to Istanbul on a one-way ticket. And, this too, is the same goal shared by most other freelance foreign correspondents.

Getting to this point, however, will be a battle for you. Like every other aspect of being a freelance foreign correspondent, you need patience, focus, and persistence.

Show Me The Money

Money is not something most freelancer journalists, especially new ones, feel comfortable discussing—especially with the people who buy their work. Workers in every other sales-focused profession love talking about money: real estate agents, plumbers, even mattress salesmen. But, by nature, freelance journalists are creatives—not businessmen. They are intimidated by placing a financial value on a product that they view in such a personal, emotional way.

After all, how can you determine the price of a story that introduces the world to a Syrian refugee who was left disfigured from a barrel bomb at her Aleppo playground? And questions like, "What is *my* value?" can be intimidating to answer, especially for anyone who's never had to sell anything but gift wrap and candles in school fundraisers.

But to be a successful freelance foreign correspondent, you must learn to bridge this divide. You must straddle the chasm between words and dollars (or euros, francs, lira, etc.).

So let's first address the most obvious question: how much money will you earn?

The price of a story varies greatly from medium to medium, news organization to news organization. But we can generally estimate the high and low ends.

Most radio reports range from $20 up to several hundred dollars. Print stories can fall within the same range. Television and multimedia video pieces that you produce, shoot, or report will earn you the higher end of several hundred dollars, and maybe even up to $1,000+ if it's a long-form or time-consuming project. And web-specific reports will generally earn you as low as $10 to several hundred dollars. Photos have around the same price points.

However, some strings instead pay you not by the piece, but by the day or hour. This arrangement often works in your favor because it usually more accurately values the work you put into a story. If you spend more time working on a long, complicated reporting project, you'll get paid more. Whereas, if you're paid a fixed rate per piece you might be paid the same amount for a piece that takes days to work on as you would with one you can whip out in an hour.

Some strings will require you to sign yearly contracts that determine the amount you'll be paid for your work for the next 12 months. Others will simply adjust the amount you'll be paid with how long they want the piece to be, or how much reporting it will involve.

You'll also want to know that the size of a news organization generally has very little to do with how much they will pay you. Don't expect that the larger the string, the better the payout. Oftentimes, it's the smaller news organizations that must value their relationships with freelancers as their primary drivers of content that pay livable rates, rather than the star strings that might come with a little prestige but little else.

Fortunately, you can expect the value of your stories to generally increase over time. If you prove to strings you are reliable, experienced, creative, and hard working, you'll be in a better position to leverage those professional skills to earn you more money for each assignment you do for them.

Not only will the value of your reporting increase, but you might also be able to package in extras with your assignment that could earn you more money. For instance, try taking your own photos or videos for your stories. Ask if your editors would like the additional content and suggest they pay you an extra fee for your work. Online news organizations especially love any multimedia content you can provide them.

Many freelancers must often subtract their expenses from what they earn. For instance, if you're based in Athens but you take a flight or ferry to a Greek island to cover the refugee crisis, you will have to consider subtracting the cost of your travel from the money you made from your reporting.

Hague-based freelance photojournalist Robert Goddyn warns many journalists end up taking on the cost of stories that involve significant travel expenses, before getting strings to accept their pitches: "They do that from their own wallet, then they try to sell it after," Goddyn says.

Sometimes, this can pay off. If you're only a short flight away from a major crisis unfolding and you've got strings you think would be ready to start buying, it's not a bad idea to get to the scene as quick as you can and start selling your work after. In most cases, you'll quickly earn back the initial expenses you paid, or will be able to convince a string to reimburse you if you are particularly helpful to them. But in other cases, especially if it's a feature story, this strategy could be financially reckless.

It's not just travel that you'll have to factor into the cost of reporting a story. If you are working on a television report, you'll need to hire a cameraman or rent your own equipment, if you don't have what your string requires. For some stories you might need to hire assistants like fixers, translators, and drivers. That often means paying those professionals in cash out of your pocket, weeks, or even months before you've received full payment for the story you worked on together from your client string.

Oftentimes, the amount you will make from a story simply won't cover the expenses you will have in reporting it, or you'll break even. In most situations, this won't be a sustainable path for you as a freelance foreign correspondent, unless you're a "trust fund baby"—a type of freelance foreign correspondent who need not worry about finances but who is bemoaned by all others.

Sometimes, though, it might be a good idea to accept an assignment or pitch a story that won't earn you enough money to cover your expenses, *if* you suspect there could be regular good-paying work that could result from a new relationship with a string. The only other reason to accept or pitch such an assignment would be non-financial. Perhaps it's a challenging story that you've always wanted to report on. In this case, do the story only for the professional or personal satisfaction, but recognize you'll have to take a financial loss.

Generally though, you should focus mainly on only accepting work that earns you a clear profit.

The "golden goose" strings are the ones that pay for your expenses like travel and even incidentals like meals and lodging costs while on assignment, and pay a living rate.

Strings like these are hard to get. And, if you do get them: never let them go! Guard them like a dragon watching a jailed princess, and always be on the lookout for other ruthless hungry freelancers eager to steal them away.

Once you've established yourself as a valuable and productive freelance foreign correspondent, you'll likely also have to turn down or cut loose other low-paying ones. When you've reached this stage in your career, you'll feel like you finally "made it." But be smart about your financial strategy.

Usually, you never want to turn down work that will make you a clear profit. However, at some point your most valuable commodity as a freelancer will be your time. So if working for a low-paying string means you won't have the time to accept regular work with a new higher paying one, you'll have to cut loose the less valuable string or negotiate a comparable raise with them. For good karma, I like to offer up the discarded string to other freelancers with whom I trust my reputation on.

However, don't jeopardize any string that regularly provides you a steady flow of income to focus only on one string that might have a big one-time payout for a time-consuming project, like a television network. If you suspect this network will rarely come calling after you initially work with them, financially it won't make much sense to work with them if it means you'll have to sacrifice any of your other more financially reliable strings.

One other way to earn another source of income is to partner with a freelance network like GRNlive. Aimed at broadcast news organizations, the company provides them with freelancers around the world for one-off assignments—usually spot news in far-flung places where those news outlets don't have any full-time or freelance journalists. The company operates almost as an agent and manager on behalf of the freelancer. It arranges work for them at the request of a news organization, and manages payment. The company also says its freelancers don't have to wait months to get paid. It pays freelancers directly a fixed rate on behalf of the client news organization. This is a handy way to earn extra money if you're in a location where you struggle to sell news, or you simply can't find many strings interested in your region. Freelance networks like GRNlive connect you to a wider pool of potential news organizations, so you're ready to work whenever an American, British, or South African news organization finds a story that interests them. However, some freelancers prefer to work directly with news organizations than through freelance networks like GRNlive. When working independently, there's no middleman you have to deal with and you can more easily negotiate higher payments for more complex reporting projects.

Freelance photojournalist Nicolas Axelrod recommends another website to help news organizations find you: blink.la. The online platform allows freelancers to constantly update their locations so media companies that quickly need to find someone to shoot a project nearby can locate and hire them easily. This is convenient for freelancers who find themselves roving entire regions like Africa or Southeast Asia. It exists as both a web and mobile app.

Regardless of how much—or how little—money you make, realize that you've already made it much farther than many other journalists trying to do the same thing you're doing. Don't discredit your hard work even if you're not yet where you want to be financially. Stay focused and appreciated what you've built for yourself along the way.

Chasing Money

The economics of freelancing change your perspective on work. Instead of mindlessly going to work each day to earn the same amount in your paycheck week after week, you learn to value every day of work. Because, you never know how long it might be until the next paycheck.

And while your journalistic work should always be your focus, you also need to make sure strings pay you on time.

The freelance community abroad—and even at home—is rife with tales of journalists who never got paid for their work. It's a sad, unfortunate reality. And it's a major hassle to track down payments when you're half a world away. But your only collections agency is you.

There are some measures you can take to make sure you get the money you are owed.

To start, use the pitch tracker that you were introduced to in the previous chapter to mark when you filed a story, and when it was published or aired. I usually like to submit an invoice (see Appendix A for a sample invoice) for my work as soon as it's filed with a string. Sometimes it might take weeks or even months before a news organization will publish or air your work. If they've accepted it, then you shouldn't have to wait even longer than what's usual to get paid.

When first accepting work from a string ask how long it takes to usually receive payment. Sometimes you'll find the rare string who will pay you on the spot for your work in cash, but usually it takes anywhere from a couple weeks to several months to see the money in your bank account. Many of the news organizations that you will work for are large, hulking behemoth bureaucracies. Their payment processes are slow and complicated. Before your first payment you will often have to fill out and submit tax and accounting forms. Keep track of when you submitted those standard boilerplate forms and to whom. If it's been at least a couple weeks from the time you filed your story and your expected date of payment, it's time to start emailing and calling your editors to politely let them know of the financial discrepancy and ask for their help.

Oftentimes, editors want nothing to do with the payment process. They feel like it isn't their responsibility to pay you; it's the finance or accounting department's. If this is the case, ask for the contact information of the person or department responsible for issuing payments to freelancers and try and work directly with them. However, any good editor knows getting their freelancers paid means keeping them happy, which means keeping them as a regular content provider.

Sometimes news organizations will have entire online payment management systems built for freelancers and other independent contractors and vendors. These can be helpful to keep track of documents and key payment or invoice dates for your records. These systems can also provide you with instant updates on the status of your payment.

If possible, you should ask for direct bank deposit options for payments. Paper checks can take a while to get issued, and having them mailed to you abroad can be a time-consuming and worrying process.

Sometimes news organizations will only issue payments to freelancers as old-fashioned paper checks mailed to your domestic home address. This is an inconvenience to you. How can you sign the check to deposit or cash it? One solution is to have a *trusted* family member or friend act as a joint account holder or your power of attorney. Obviously there are risks associated with both of these options. A long-distance dispute with this financial partner could leave you penniless. However, it might be a wise investment of your time to secure this kind of arrangement prior to your departure from home. For instance, your mother or father could sign and deposit the checks on your behalf under both of these arrangements. Mobile checking apps make this even easier. Your financial representative simply signs the check, snaps a picture, and hits deposit without ever having to stand in line at a bank. Almost instantly you'll be able to see the status of the deposit thousands of miles away. Joint checking account holders will have the most access to your money, but a power of attorney will be able to also sign other documents on your behalf. Some state bar associations offer free power of attorney forms that only need to be completed by both parties and notarized.

Also, even if your story is killed or they never publish or air it for whatever reason, I believe you are still entitled to full payment. If, for some reason, they are unsatisfied with your reporting you should ask for guidance on what you can do to address the issue they have with your work. At the very least, if they don't like your work and there's nothing you can do to satisfy them, you should request some sort of "kill fee" if you can't get them to pay the full rate for the story. Usually these kill fees are significantly lower than what you'd normally get for your work, but if they aren't willing to pay you the full amount it's better than nothing. Oftentimes, producing work that never sees the light of day or is unsatisfactory to your editors will end your professional relationship with them. However, sometimes, it's not your fault. Perhaps they wanted you to pursue an angle that never existed. Or maybe no sources for the story they assigned you were available to be interviewed for the piece under the tight deadline your editor required, so you used tertiary sources that didn't necessarily meet the expectations of your editors. Whatever the issue is with the story try to stay optimistic and salvage whatever working relationship you can with the string, unless its more trouble than it's worth.

Finally, if the string has become unresponsive to your payment requests over a period of several months, email, fax, or mail a final demand letter. In it, explicitly outline your attempts to reach them and receive payment, how much you are owed, and perhaps even add in a late fee. (With all of my invoices, I like to include a note that late payments will incur late fees, just as any collections agency would.) You might also want to allude to taking legal action. Most likely you won't ever go down the path through the courts—because you're 3,000 miles away and it's more trouble than it may be worth for a couple of hundred bucks. But you do have every right to take the issue to small claims court where you generally don't even need an attorney. Organizations such as the National Writers' Union can also help with payment grievances if you've reached this point.

No matter how the situation is resolved, never work for strings who don't pay again and warn all your freelance colleagues to do the same—you would've appreciated the same.

Taxes

No matter where you are in the world, you'll likely have to pay taxes on your earning abroad as a freelance foreign correspondent. If you're used to having your employer deduct taxes every pay period, you'll be shocked when you go a year without doing it and then ending up owing thousands at tax time.

Most of your strings will simply issue a check for the full amount they owe you, and then perhaps issue you a statement at the end of the year to help you calculate what you owe in taxes to the government. Be sure to keep track of these forms. In the U.S. they often come as IRS W2 or 1099 forms. To help prevent a surprise at the end of the year ask the accounting departments of your strings if they will deduct any estimated taxes that you owe—just like they normally would for any of their part-time employees. However, it's possible they consider you in a different category of worker and this is not possible.

In this case, it's wise to consult with a personal financial advisor, accountant, or other financial expert. They can give you an estimate on your tax obligation. U.S. citizens must pay taxes on all earning worldwide, but this isn't necessarily the case with citizens of other countries. If you do have a tax obligation to meet, you'll have to set aside part of what you think you might owe at the end of the year from every paycheck. However, this will be hard when it's not done for you. You'll want to use as much money as you've got coming in. But you might be able to arrange an automatic deduction from one of your bank accounts to another that can be used for tax purposes later.

In some cases, you might also be able to deduct your businesses expenses from your taxes. According to the free-to-join Freelancers' Union, some of the most common expenses you can deduct include domain and web hosting for your site advertising your services as an independent journalist, apps, and online tools you use to do your job like Adobe Creative Cloud and Dropbox, and office supplies like notebooks and pens.[1]

Here again, a trusted financial advisor or accountant could also instruct you with better insight on how to manage your money while overseas and stretch your earnings as a freelancer. (Time to reach out to all those long-lost accounting majors you used to be friends with!)

Financial Karate

To survive as a freelancer, you not only have to make money, but you have to learn to spend it wisely. You must become an expert in the dark art of penny pinching and financial kung fu.

When you're considering spending any money in a professional capacity—say a new DSLR camera to tackle new work shooting photos for strings—you must evaluate the potential of that expense as an actual investment.

You must ask yourself: "Will this purchase help me make more money, or will I at least recover the cost of it?" If all of your work as a freelance journalist is writing for print, but you've gotten a commitment from a string that they'd buy any videos you shot with your new DSLR camera on a weekly basis and pay you twice as much than for a standard print story then that piece of equipment is worth its investment. In several weeks you'll recoup the cost of the camera, and then begin to earn more money at a faster rate.

If however, you drop $5,000 on a new camera, and it takes six months just to earn $400 from a couple of video stories you pitched, it's best to concentrate on other media that don't require you to own such costly equipment. Or find a way to rent the equipment at an affordable rate and work your way up to finding more strings who have more consistent video needs from your location.

One way to make your investments in expenses go farther is to maximize your story pitches. If you're doing a costly reporting trip, try to sell the same story or different versions of it to several strings so you can recoup your travel expenses more quickly. But try not to sell the same story to competing media. For example, don't sell a video report to ABC if you already sold the story to CBS. If you suspect another string in a competing medium would be interested in the story and you want to make extra money, simply ask for the permission of the editor you first pitched it to and also let the editor at the second string know where else the report will show up if they accept the story. However, you'll likely have an easier time getting away with this strategy if you instead sell the video report to ABC and then a web version of the story to BuzzFeed. You might also not run into any trouble if you sell your pitches to the same media, but in different countries like ABC in the U.S. and CBC in Canada. One more method is to pitch one story focused on one angle from your reporting trip, but the same story with a different angle and maybe a few of the same elements to a similar competing string. Whatever way you can, try to find ways to stretch the money you make on any costly professional investment.

Finally, make the most out of the professional relationships you establish in your country. If you know another freelancer is traveling to the same story you are, suggest to them that you share expenses like cabs or even hotels. Also considering reaching out to the foreign correspondents club in your country to find out where the best reporter- and budget-friendly spots to stay in are located.

Clearly, you'll also want to be conservative with your living and personal expenses as well. Find any way you can to save money. We've already discussed the importance of affordable rent, transportation, food, and the other basics of living internationally. But one thing you can do to easily help reduce your expenses is to find the most efficient way to access your money.

If you are staying somewhere for the long term, consider opening a local bank account. This could offer you several advantages, including allowing your strings to directly wire money into your account that you can easily access in-country with very few barriers. In fact, some strings prefer to wire their payments, but I suggest you ask for them to cover the fee you incur to accept the money internationally if this is the case.

You should also look into getting fee-free ATM and credit cards for your accounts back home. Most ATM cards from banks will charge you a few dollars to withdraw money at ATMs that aren't their own. Most North American banks, for instance, don't have many of their own ATMs abroad, unless you're a member of a large international bank like HSBC. Many credit card users also incur a small fee for using their cards for international purchases. You should ask your bank at home what low-cost or fee-free international ATM and credit card options are available to you, or simply do some research online through reputable financial sources. Whatever financial method you choose to access your money from home abroad, being able to do this with little or no cost to you is much better than suffering through high fees or poor exchange rates with money changers.

No matter how successful you are as a freelance foreign correspondent in making money, you could still end up in a financial ditch if you don't know how to spend and manage that money wisely. You'll also earn a new appreciation for money. You recognize it's no longer something you show up to work for for one day and get a paycheck at the end of the week. It's something you fight every day to earn. You value every assignment and you celebrate every paycheck. Making a living for yourself when the odds are literally stacked against you in every possible way is beyond gratifying. Your survival, and even your thriving existence, in countries where millions perhaps live in desperate poverty will reveal a type of self-reliance and entrepreneurialism you never knew existed.

Note

1 Murphy, Kendra. "The Ultimate List of Freelancer Tax Deductions." Freelancers Union. January 28, 2015, https:// www.freelancersunion.org/blog/2015/01/28/ultimate-list-freelancer-tax-deductions/. Accessed September 27, 2015.

6

NEW MEDIA

At this point, after you've come to terms with the financial realities of working as a freelance foreign correspondent you probably aren't feeling so great. In fact, you probably feel hopeless and literally worthless as a journalist.

However, one major change in media has given new hope to freelance journalists: new media. Online news organizations have made a career as a freelance foreign correspondent possible for more journalists than at any other time.

New media have "really created some new opportunities," says Trevor Knoblich, digital director for the U.S.-based Online News Association. "We're also seeing some real investments" in foreign correspondence from online news sites like VICE and BuzzFeed. Each takes advantage of strong financial investments from traditional media players like 21st Century Fox and NBCUniversal, respectively.

Multimedia storytelling and advances in digital technology have meant an explosion of online-only news outlets interested in stories all over the world. Not only that, but finally many of these web-only news platforms are beginning to find value in professional journalists and actually pay them for their work!

These digital media opportunities are especially beneficial for freelance foreign correspondents. While legacy media are retreating from investing in foreign news, new media are doing the opposite.

"There's a lot of renewed energy," Knoblich says.

Many freelancers these days report exclusively for online media. They curate and aggregate content, but also tie together everything from drones to maps with new narrative storytelling styles. We're also starting to see the web's video revolution. News organizations are investing millions in short-form videos and long-form documentary-style reporting. Social media have changed the way we cover, find, and share news. And data-driven reporting has found a new home off the front pages of newspapers onto the front of websites like Vox and FiveThirtyEight.

For a freelance foreign correspondent, this means there are more opportunities and more ways than ever for you to tell and sell stories. New media have made reporting independently sustainable for many more people.

Reporting for New Media

According to the American Press Institute, the average American uses four devices to get his news. While 87 percent of Americans follow news on television, more than half access news content on cell phones and about one in 10 uses smart TVs and other devices.[1]

In the UK for instance, the British government's 2014 news consumption report found 41 percent of adults there use internet or apps for news, growing from 32 percent just a year prior.[2] That's more than the number of UK adults reading printed newspapers.

The number of places to find news is growing: e-readers, Xbox and PlayStation, and iPhones are complementing traditional news sources like radio, TV, and newspapers. This means there is more space and opportunities to feed the news beast across platforms. There is a greater opportunity for free-lance journalists—even foreign correspondents—to work.

But users of new media are not necessarily the same people who consume legacy media.

New media users also tend to skew younger, compared to their legacy media counterparts. A 2013 Gallup poll found more than a quarter of American adults 18 to 29 prefer internet-based sources of news, compared to just 6 percent of those over 65.[3] An overwhelming majority of that older age group—68 percent—say TV is their primary source of news, according to the poll.

Since the audience for online media is generally younger than that of other news sources, you'll find much different audience-tailored news content in the digital world. Just consider some of the headlines on BuzzFeed News, for example: "This Puerto Rican Dude Created a Donald Trump Salsa Anthem to Show Not All Latinos Hate Him." Even older news organization like Foreign Policy are trying to get hip with online stories like, "Britain to Jamaica: In Lieu of Reparations, Here's a Prison." Some of these stories are written as if they're the love children of the *New York Post* and TMZ. Generally, there's nothing wrong with these types of story. They're engaging, humorous, fun to read, and enlightening. They're just written in a different style than what you'd perhaps find in the *New York Times*, and for a different audience.

"I'm always surprised how old-media feeling the headlines in the newspaper read, compared to the [search-engine-] optimized stuff that goes on top of my U.S. online stories," says Patrick St. Michel, who freelances in Japan.

Because online audiences can be significantly different from print audiences, you might have to craft your pitches and reporting differently to new media, than to old.

Sometimes, this means your writing style will be different.

"I'd say in general, I find I can be a bit more casual when writing for online publications, though that tends to be for entertainment-focused sites which might already have been a bit more lax," St. Michel says. "Newspapers remain extremely popular here in Japan, and I have to be a bit more 'serious' when writing for the *Japan Times*."

But reporting for online media means you can often pursue stories legacy media are too apprehensive to tell. This allows you the opportunity to pitch more unconventional stories such as Sweden's boom in sexually transmitted diseases or spending a day with the kingpins of China's estimated $1 billion human organ-trafficking rings. Enjoy this freedom, because in many senses new media have allowed a new Renaissance for journalism where content is allowed to break free from the stuffy confines of legacy newsrooms and explore new ways of telling stories.

"I like being able to cover a story in many different ways," says Colin Cosier, an Ethiopia-based Australian freelance foreign correspondent who describes himself as a "cross-format" journalist.

Now, this doesn't mean you have to resign yourself to telling only made-for-the-web offbeat stories or listicles, and writing cute headlines. Instead, new media are especially effective at telling a complicated, impactful story, especially when it's paired with multimedia content.

In fact, let's review a piece in GlobalPost that takes on a story that would otherwise be neglected by legacy media:

"Myanmar's Mine Raiders: Living on Stolen Dirt"
By Patrick Winn
May 1, 2013

KYISINTAUNG MOUNTAIN, Myanmar—When the quarry guards show up, you run like hell.

You drop your sacks of pilfered dirt and scramble down the steep rim of the copper mine. When you reach the base, you keep running, bounding over pools awash in sulfuric acid. Be careful: Plenty of boys before you have tumbled in and snapped limbs.

Do not look back.

Do not stop sprinting until you slip unseen into the village.

These are the rules Ko Ko Aung learned as a child, even before he quit school at the age of 11. He is now a scraggly 15.

He is not yet a man because a man, he explains, can carry four sacks of stolen, crumbled earth down the mountain. "Three sacks use all of my energy," he says. But he is nimble in his youth.

"I know how to run with all my bones."

"When I climb the hill, I'm only thinking, 'When are the guards coming after me?' Even strong men have to stay alert," Ko Ko Aung says. "If you're caught, they throw you in a car. They take away your dirt. Then they put you in jail."

Ko Ko Aung insists he's not a thief. "I'm only taking dirt," he says.

But that pebbly mess belongs to the mine's owner and its operator: Union of Myanmar Economic Holdings, a secretive military investment wing, and Wanbao, a subsidiary of China's largest state-owned weapons manufacturer.

Each morning, Ko Ko Aung trudges across the treeless moonscape behind his family shack. He scales a high, man-made dune composed of soil scooped out by cranes in the interior and dumped around the periphery by behemoth trucks. The trucks' tires alone are nearly triple Ko Ko Aung's height.

To Ko Ko Aung's family, and hundreds of others living on the mine's fringe, the rocky soil sustains life. Dug out from the mineral-rich mountain, it is strewn with copper ore.

With 40 days, some sulfuric acid and painstaking effort, they can produce a pile of maroon rocks that twinkle in the light. Fed into a smelter, the pebbles cook into a heavy brick of low-purity copper. It is nasty work. Squatting over stones doused in sulfuric acid singes the nostrils, makes the eyes run hot with stinging tears and slowly gnaws at their health. But only when the villagers sell these bricks for about $40 profit are they able to buy luxuries such as shoes or meat.

"The mine doesn't even need the dirt. We do," Ko Ko Aung says. "But they call us thieves. Even though we no longer have our land and no other way to survive."

What Democracy Looks Like

Ko Ko Aung is an unwitting foot soldier in Myanmar's great struggle to transform from a despotic state lorded over by generals into a freer society that cedes basic rights to peasants.

A movement initiated by ruling military elite to reinvent the troubled nation as a legit democracy is the subject of global attention, and much hype. In the last year or so, hundreds of political prisoners were freed, the press has been largely uncensored and poor villagers have grown emboldened enough to rally against powerful interests. The democracy champion Aung San Suu Kyi, lionized globally for resisting the generals' tyranny, has even joined the government as an elected lawmaker.

These liberties have also turned this mining region into an unruly protest zone.

Long-held grievances over the mine's land confiscations and environmental wreckage have given rise to monk-led rallies. And though they are finally free to openly agitate for the mine's closure, some of the authorities' old habits are dying hard. A Nov. 29 raid on protest camps left roughly 100 monks and civilians badly burned by lobbed white phosphorus munitions, a tool of war.

With tensions high, the government of President Thein Sein, a former high-ranking general, dispatched Aung San Suu Kyi to tame local anger through a commission investigating anti-mine grievances.

But in a sign of times changed, the leader best known for her uncompromising resistance to generals' subjugation has urged villagers' to patiently tolerate the mine's environmental damage and trust the military-owned project to eventually pour profits towards repairing the natural habitat.

This trust, however, is widely regarded as unearned. In the eyes of many, the Nobel Laureate's siding with a massive military development project over poor villagers has bruised her image—an outcome her camp regarded as inevitable amid her transition from confined icon to lawmaker.

"She's a politician now," said Nyan Win, her spokesman and close confidante. "Maybe her reputation has taken some effect."

Hollowed Out

In the case of Ko Ko Aung's family, the toll on nature and health drains the strength of an already ill and poorly nourished clan of grey-market coppersmiths.

"Bad coughs. Pains in our chests. I don't even know the names of all these diseases," Ko Ko Aung says. "But we have sore throats and find it hard to breathe."

Ko Ko Aung pinches a leafy wad stuffed with betel nut, jams it in his mouth and works his jaw. The rush comes on within seconds. Crimson liquid pools at the corners of his mouth. He looks as if he's just gnawed the head off a bat.

A gentle narcotic that turns saliva red, betel nut is Myanmar's preferred pick-me-up. Ko Ko Aung began chewing it to stave off the fatigue of working seven days a week. But he became doubly fond of the stimulant when he realized it masked the taste of acidic dust. "It erases the bitter taste," he says. "If I don't chew it, my mouth aches."

Ko Ko Aung has a fantasy. He would like to become a doctor. But when he announces this out loud, his sisters and a gaggle of neighbors burst into laughter. It sounds absurd coming from a sixth-grade dropout, his legs caked in dirt and palms marred by rubbery callouses.

He tries to talk over their giggling.

"Inside the mine, they spray rocks with acid, the wind blows and the dust gets in our insides," Ko Ko Aung says. "People here are so unhealthy and I would like to cure them."

The laughter fades. "He's right," says Moe Moe Win, a 22-year-old sister of Ko Ko Aung and mother of two. "This place is filthy. The well water here is so bad that it makes vegetables change color."

For more than a decade, they have lived among the mine waste piled around their village. Here, they make copper in a forsaken, otherworldly place. Pushed from their land decades ago to make way for the mine, they have constructed wooden shacks, with sagging roofs made of palm fronds, on a dirt plane strewn with caustic mine waste. They are too broke to move, Ko Ko Aung says.

Barefoot kids toddle around pools of liquid treated with acid. Some are put to work by the age of 10 and have wet coughs to show for it. Many try to fulfill mining duties while still attending school up the road. There, they have learned a few English words: teacher, I love you, dog and Justin Bieber.

The government has divided the bleak stretch where the villagers make copper at the mine's base into an invisible checkerboard of 50-square-meter plots. Each plot rents for $3.50 per year. The land is too contaminated for vegetation. Wind comes in hard, dusty gusts. You yawn, you eat dust.

Generations of Misrule

Moe Moe Win recalls the unexplained 2009 death of Ko Htay's granddaughter who, at the age of four, "turned yellow and kept vomiting until she died. "I can't tell you what happened. We have no medical knowledge," she says. "But we all breathe polluted air and sleep around polluted dirt."

Their father, Ko Htay, believes he is slowly succumbing to the toxins. "My heart, my kidneys, my lungs," he says, tracing a finger around his concave chest. "All of them are sore."

Ko Htay speaks through a gummy maw studded with a few stubborn incisors. His 59-year-old body is a skeletal ode to resilience. By the standards of backcountry Myanmar, among the poorest and most isolated places in Southeast Asia, he is an old man.

He got this far by making outlaw coppersmiths of his eight children before they hit puberty. Most are now married off and struggling to nourish kids of their own. Ko Htay is too old to scale waste dunes or outrun security guards. So he adopted Ko Ko Aung, the orphan son of a drifter long dead from liver disease.

He blames generations of misrule in Myanmar for turning him into a sickly, landless man relying on a teenage boy for survival.

Even before 19th-century British colonists invaded "Upper Burma," as it was then known, Ko Htay's ancestors farmed 20 acres outside a trading outpost called Monywa. They managed to retain the croplands through a chaotic period following the 1948 English exodus, when the national army fought back bandits and revolutionaries.

By the mid-1960s, Myanmar was settling into the iron military rule that influences its government to this day. Under the banner of socialism, the army began swallowing up privately owned businesses and land en masse. "The army confiscated our farm in 1966 and offered no compensation," Ko Htay says. "It is now inside the mine's restricted zone. My ancestral land is now buried under heaps of [mine waste]."

Myanmar is once again undergoing a great upheaval. After five decades of totalitarianism, the nation's style of rule softened in the last two years into a more internationally palatable system: parliamentary governance under the army's sway. Western sanctions are fading away. The state has loosened its chokehold on the economy.

But mining remains the military-steered nation's top foreign cash source after oil and gas ventures. Lacking top-flight mining knowhow, the military shares the lucre with outsiders skilled at extracting Myanmar's natural bounty. These deals are cash cows for Myanmar's generals.

Foreign mining entities are currently undertaking $2.3 billion worth of projects inside the resource-rich nation. Much of that cash will go toward extracting copper from the region Ko Ko Aung calls home.

In 1998, the year in which Ko Ko Aung was likely born (he does not know his birth date), the Canada-based mining firm Ivanhoe (now Turquoise Hill Resources) extracted what commodities traders call "grade A cathode copper" from pits behind his village.

In league with Myanmar's ruling junta, Ivanhoe had embarked on the "Monywa Copper Project." Though other foreign mining operations had plied these mountains before—namely a Yugoslavian outfit with less advanced techniques—Ivanhoe would pour more than $100 million toward detonating, digging and dissolving their way to the billion-plus tons of copper buried in the region's hills.

The once-verdant mountains rising above Ko Ko Aung's village began to shrink. As more and more farms were buried beneath mine waste, more families resorted to looting debris for illicit coppersmithing.

Today, the twin mountains known as Sabetaung and Kyisintaung are reduced to bald craters, squeezed hollow like blackheads. "They get a little smaller every year," Ko Ko Aung says. "Sabetaung is almost entirely gone."

China Steps In

Squabbles with the junta eventually compelled Ivanhoe to sell off its stake in the mine. China's Norinco, through a subsidiary called Myanmar Wanbao, stepped in as the junta's foreign partner in 2009. The company has since vowed to invest nearly $1.4 billion over 30 years to draw out the remaining copper reserves, which will be divided between the government, the military's chief investment wing and Norinco's subsidiaries.

Much of Norinco's share is expected to supply China's People's Liberation Army. The metal is used for everything from casing bullets to wiring tanks. But the defense consortium's clientele network is extensive, and its copper will likely end up scattered around the world.

Norinco produces the world's most widespread AK-47-style rifle. Its Remington shotgun clone remains popular in the United States. It also manufactures radios, toys and a myriad other products that include copper as well.

But Norinco also has a habit of riling the US federal government. A 1996 sting caught Norinco employees helping smuggle 2,000 assault rifles to US agents posing as mafia. Sales of super-strength steel to an Iranian missile facility brought years of anti-Norinco sanctions beginning in 2003.

Still, anyone can acquire the copper Norinco extracts from the hills behind Ko Ko Aung's shack. Via forms downloadable from one of its web sites, the defense consortium sells high-purity copper by the slab. Offers below 100 metric tons—market price: over $650,000—are not accepted.

Drinking Drywall

Being thirsty in Ko Ko Aung's village, Kankone, is not advised. Cups of water from the village wells are as refreshing as a slurp from the ocean. Though visibly clear, the water is a briny mix that makes the tongue recoil.

Even Moe Moe Win, whose family business involves handling rocks dunked in acid, draws the line at drinking from the village well. "It's not good enough for my kids," she says. "We send Ko Ko Aung to get water from the monastery two kilometers (1.25 miles) up the road." Another villager, 30-year-old Kaba Chit, says the water quality went south about 10 years back. "That's when it turned bitter" he says, "and started giving everyone diarrhea."

Approached at random, villagers living around the mine spout a litany of grievances against the operation. Among them: controlled detonations that spook livestock and crack temple spires; sore throats and eyes that never seem to heal. The mine has become a catch-all for accusations involving cancer and common rashes, birth defects and infertility—although the villagers' livelihood, involving metal-laden rock and a dangerous, corrosive acid, could also be the culprit.

But the villagers' loudest objection by far is that the mine—somehow, at some point—spoiled the water supply.

"It's not just that the taste is bitter," says Pyn Nyar Zaw Da, a monk whose temple is frequently rocked by detonations inside the mine. "It's the crops too," he says. "Our yields are getting lower and lower. There's too much waste in the groundwater. How are the villagers supposed to eat?"

Wanbao's Response

Accustomed to these complaints, Wanbao has rebuttals at the ready. "These claims are untrue," says Liu Xiaoduan, deputy manager of Wanbao Mining's operations department. "Water protection is one of the highest goals of our company."

But unpublished water sampling data, obtained by GlobalPost and analyzed by environmental experts in the US, reinforces what villagers have known for years: The water drawn from many wells outside the mine is repellant.

"Think drinking drywall mixed with water," says Kendra Zamzow, an environmental geochemist with the Center for Science in Public Participation, a Montana-based non-profit that researches the impact of mines.

According to Wanbao, the mine is an idyllic place where "many visitors are in awe of jumping deer, flocks of geese and various ducks, as well as of the waters teaming with countless varieties of aquatic life" inside the 5,600-acre mining site. The mine's promotional imagery features dump trucks posed before sunsets, villagers happily bathing beside a waste pile and a duckling symbolically snuggled up to an owl.

But large-scale copper mining is a messy, inherently precarious endeavor. Advanced operations such as Wanbao's mine spread copper-rich ore over hundreds of acres—called "leach pads"—where stones soak in sulfuric acid. All that prevent toxins from seeping into groundwater are underground sheets of synthetic plastic.

Wanbao insists its water monitoring regimen is exhaustive and legitimized by outside auditors from Singapore. The firm has published stats on acid mist detection and water-monitoring boreholes.

The latest government report, helmed by the globally known dissident-turned-parliamentarian Aung San Suu Kyi, decreed in March that the mine exudes no toxic discharge. But it pushed the mine's operators to step up environmental protections, offer more jobs to locals and hike payments to farmers forced to evacuate their land for future mine expansions.

When Suu Kyi visited the region in March as the report was released—a mission to tame local anger against the mine—Ko Ko Aung watched her greet villagers from afar. "I waved at her from the acid field," he says.

To date, the only published analyses of the mining area's water supplies have been commissioned by either Myanmar's government or the mine's foreign operators.

But GlobalPost obtained lab results from samples collected by two Myanmar-based environmental groups: Mandalay's Seinyaungso and Yangon's Global Green Group. The groups had sent the results to both Myanmar's president and Suu Kyi in hopes of convincing authorities of the mine region's contamination. "We mailed copies to them months ago, said Devi Thant Cin, president of the Global Green Group. "Neither responded."

The samples suggest the truth about the mine's environmental degradation floats somewhere between villagers' loose claims and the mine operators' stiff denials.

The worst-case scenario—acid leakage into groundwater—appears to be held at bay, says Zamzow, who reviewed the lab results at GlobalPost's request. Collected in Kankone village, a nearby makeshift mining site and a stream in which liquid mine waste is drained, the water samples all show normal pH levels. "There's nothing here that indicates acid drainage," she said.

The chalky, gag-inducing taste, she said, comes from the overwhelming quantity of sulfates in the groundwater. Both the United States Environmental Protection Agency and the World Health Organization warn against drinking water with 250 milligrams of sulfate per liter, and set 500 as a "maximum contaminant level."

Various samples collected from public wells in Ko Ko Aung's village indicate sulfate milligram-per-liter counts in excess of these standards: 816, 653 and 451. Labs in Mandalay, where the samples were processed, described the water as "chemically unpotable."

Drinking water with these sulfate levels isn't deadly, according to EPA studies. But sulfates are a natural laxative. Diarrhea, a common illness in Kankone village, is a drain on adults already weakened by overwork and malnutrition. Sulfates pose even bigger risks to babies. "I don't think the water is toxic," Zamzow says. "But it sure looks like it would make you sick."

Sulfate-heavy groundwater is common around large-scale mine sites where excavation is deep enough to disturb earth near the aquifer.

"You have to look at the mine's expansion, how deep it goes and how long it would take water to flow to these wells. With some aquifers, it can take years," Zamzow says. "But it sounds like the mine is the source of these water problems."

"Self-Inflicted Poisoning"

During four weeks of contact with GlobalPost, Wanbao officials agreed to three different face-to-face interviews: one at the mine, one in Yangon and one in Beijing. All were cancelled at the last minute. Eventually, the Norinco subsidiary would only agree to communicate through e-mail.

In detailing Wanbao's benevolence, Xiaoduan noted that it had created 2,200 jobs for Myanmar's citizens, and is now offering jobs to farming families relocated by its massive expansion—at $3.50-per-day, an above-average salary for unskilled labor. He also mentions sponsoring schoolchildren, and building a new community library filled with donated books. "At Wanbao," he writes, "we care greatly for the wellbeing of the men, women and children who live in our local areas."

As for the bane of kids from coppersmith families: guards in Wanbao uniforms pursuing them time and time again?

"Myanmar Wanbao never chased down or detained any locals who . . . just passed through the mine's outskirts. These are false claims," Xiaoduan writes. The firm, however, has "asked the assistance of the local government to help in alerting people of the dangers to themselves of entering the mine area." Mine waste is often laced with heavy metals and dangerous chemicals, posing risks to humans who come in contact with them.

Mu Zaw Oo, an elder brother of Ko Ko Aung who has been nabbed more than once, describes a much more hands-on experience. "We go through three pairs of shoes per year running from them," he says. Muddy socks are visible through a worn gash in his Chinese-made imitation Chuck Taylors. The going payment for release from jail, the family says, is about $58. "If I have to dive down the mountain," he says, "I dive."

The mine's operators are highly aware of the rogue coppersmiths on the perimeter. Both Ivanhoe and Wanbao have denied a role in their livelihoods: The village coppersmiths are depicted as a tragic nuisance, feeding off 370 acres worth of dregs left behind by a former Yugoslavian operator, RTB Bor, which abandoned the mine site in the 1990s.

The current and former operators—along with Myanmar's authorities—insist that any water pollution in the mining zone can be blamed on illicit coppersmiths like Ko Ko Aung. "They take raw acid from the leaching heap and process copper . . . this is unsafe for health," Ko Ko Myint, the mine's environmental affairs manager, recently told the Yangon-based *Myanmar Times*. "They keep pots of acid near their houses and wells."

Ivanhoe's reports describe their trade as "unauthorized, unregulated hand mining . . . employing crude and hazardous improvised methods to recover small amounts of residual copper that they sell to middlemen buyers to supplement meager incomes." Wanbao's 2012–2013 report laments their "self-inflicted poisoning" and vows to seek "full cooperation with local and national authorities" in relocating these farmers-turned-coppersmiths to uncontaminated farmlands.

"I love my native land," Ko Ko Aung says, "but I hate staying in this place." He fears that the caustic dust and acid fumes are draining his youth. "It's risky," he says. He dreams of leaving this bleakness behind and starting anew. But his family, landless and dead broke, are trapped in place, he says.

For now, in lieu of evicting these families—blamed for polluting the land, and pitied for polluting their own insides—the government charges them rent to ply a wasteland at the mine's edge.

But the waste dunes towering over Ko Htay's acid pits are only growing higher. He suspects their eviction is nigh. "Last time I tried to pay at the township office," he says, "they waved me off." Without a farm to till, or pits to extract copper, he fears the worst for his family. "I am too old. But maybe my children could get a job inside the mine."

A comically oversized, counterfeit Quiksilver trucker cap on Ko Ko Aung's head obscures his expression under its brim. But it appears that his father's suggestion has unnerved him.

"The people that built this project, I would rather just drive them out," says Ko Ko Aung, his teeth stained pomegranate from betel nut. "I can't do that. But I still think what I do is right and what they do is wrong."

The reporter for this story, Patrick Winn, does a fine job of weaving together several themes like political corruption, economic destitution, and environmental degradation. To introduce us to these issues, Winn finds characters to guide us through the story. Like many good print and digital stories, he finds unique ways to describe those characters, like Ko Ko Aung's "comically oversized, counterfeit Quiksilver trucker cap." He also vividly describes the terrible conditions villagers experience while smelting copper wiring, "Squatting over stones doused in sulfuric acid singes the nostrils, makes the eyes run hot with stinging tears and slowly gnaws at their health." Winn also uses the mine as a symbol of the interplay among the story's themes amid falling hopes of the Burmese for promised national change. He also connects the story back to the West linking the mine's copper to Canada and the U.S. And, finally, he writes in the present tense—something that would be slightly unusual for traditional print journalism—effectively drawing readers into the moment. Subtle techniques like these make the story feel just a little more authentic and relevant, while weaving a strong narrative into the story.

"You cannot lose sight of the narrative," whether you're writing for print, online or broadcast, according to Knoblich. "If you've got a really strong narrative, then people will stick with you."

A strong narrative is especially important when you're trying to carry a reader through a long piece like Winn's.

Uniting Multimedia

Experimenting with many elements of multimedia to advance your reporting will also make your work stand out.

Online storytelling offers many of opportunities for digital information to be presented in a dynamic way, according to Knoblich.

In the following BuzzFeed News story, the reporter, Mike Giglio found ways to make the web work for him. The story includes many pictures of the actual smuggling deals and processes ISIS uses to smuggle oil out of Syria and earn cash. One photo included with the story online actually shows money for the oil changing hands. The story also includes an embedded video shot on a cell phone, apparently of men carrying ISIS oil drums across the border to Turkey and back into Syria.

The story also features many links to help readers go deeper. It references previous BuzzFeed stories on ISIS, as well as the reporting of other news organizations. The piece also includes a link to an emailed statement from Turkish energy officials hosted on DocumentCloud as a PDF.

Giglio employed many traditional reporting techniques like framing a story around the experience of central characters, reaching out to many sides to get a clearer picture of the issue, and including data to bolster the report. But he also used multimedia elements to stretch the impact of his storytelling, and allowed readers to go farther in the story if they choose.

Take a look at how the text of his story is written to complement the additional elements that are provided online.

"This is how ISIS Smuggles Oil"
BuzzFeed, Inc. © 2014. All rights reserved. Used with permission.
By Mike Giglio
November 3, 2014

BESASLAN, Turkey—This town on the Turkish–Syrian border is covered in trash. Residents refuse to let any outsiders—even garbagemen—inside. What makes Besaslan more guarded than the other grim towns lining what has become one of the world's most dangerous borders sits at the end of a winding dirt road: oil.

The oil brings Omar to town weekly, huddling with grease-covered men to negotiate the purchase of faded, 17-gallon drums. A Syrian in his thirties, Omar was once a proud rebel in his country's civil war. Now he's a merchant in the trade that bankrolls the extremists who hijacked it: the Islamic State of Iraq and Syria, or ISIS. The militants can make more than $1 million a day selling oil from fields captured in eastern Syria. But the way this shadowy trade works on the ground remains largely unknown.

On a recent Saturday, about 100 drums of oil were clustered at the center of a dusty lot. Omar got a price of $1.11 a liter, 42% cheaper than the standard diesel rate. This was the oil's first stop in Turkey. After ISIS drilled it inside Syria, middlemen delivered it to the Syrian border opposite Besaslan, where it was pumped into pipes buried underground. On their end of the pipes, the traders in Besaslan filled new drums. Men like Omar bought the oil from the lot and delivered it to local Turkish businessmen, who sold it secretly to gas stations or set up illegal filling stops. While Omar negotiated, a wiry man used a hose to fill a hidden oil tank beneath a white minibus. Oil drums were also packed inside buses like this or crammed into cars like the one that brought Omar to Besaslan, a minivan fit for a soccer mom.

Many cash-strapped residents take part in the dangerous business—and spotters walked the streets, keeping watch for police. Men on motorbikes peered into the van's tinted windows as it rolled back out of town toward the Turkish city of Reyhanli. The trip to Besaslan may have marked the first time a foreign journalist witnessed oil-smuggling at its source in Turkey since ISIS launched its shock offensive in Iraq this summer, sparking a global push to find and stop its revenue streams.

Turkey is a focal point in the new international fight against ISIS. Its porous, 565-mile border has been a gateway for the foreign extremists who fill the ISIS ranks—and with sky-high domestic fuel prices, it has been a key market for the oil that funds ISIS. In recent months, the government has vowed to crack down on illicit oil, and police have targeted smuggling routes, seizing oil drums and digging up pipelines. But the lot in Besaslan showed that the trade is still alive. Omar, who asked to use this pseudonym to protect his safety, also provided photo evidence of the Besaslan operation, snapped secretly on his smartphone—and a video that appeared to show oil-smuggling at a second location a short drive away.

Other sources involved in smuggling Syrian oil into Turkey said that it continued elsewhere along the border on a far greater scale. This testimony—from smugglers and businessmen who have done it themselves—provides a rare look behind the curtain of the trade that has helped make ISIS the world's richest extremists. "Before, now, and in the future, ISIS is smuggling oil into Turkey," said one of the businessmen involved, who spoke on the condition that he not be named. "And the border guards close their eyes."

Omar got his start by tying oil drums to a rope and hauling them across the border himself.

The Turkey–Syria border had been rife with oil-smuggling long before the uprising broke out in March 2011. As one Turkish smuggler remembered, all it took was the "permission" of the gendarmerie, the Turkish paramilitary force that controls the border, in the form of small bribes. A third-generation smuggler from a family with deep roots in the trade, he recounted filling cars rigged with hidden tanks at the cheaper gas stations in Syria and then driving back to Turkey when he was just a teen.

The trade erupted in the chaos of Syria's war, which began in late 2011. Rebel groups targeted oil resources from the regime in battles often overshadowed by higher-profile fronts in the war—namely in the provinces of Raqqa and Deir Ezzor, where there were refineries and oil fields. Strapped for cash, the rebels smuggled some of the oil to buyers in Turkey, whose government was one of the Syrian opposition's main backers, having already opened its borders to activists, fighters, and refugees. It was a booming business by the time Omar joined in early 2013, tired of struggling to feed his wife and kids on a fighter's small salary.

In the evenings, Omar would receive a call from a commander in the Free Syrian Army (FSA), the U.S.-backed rebel coalition, telling him to head to the Syrian side of the border. Over in Turkey, the gendarmerie would clear a path in the hills, lighting it with the floodlights on their armored trucks. Back in Syria, a small army of vehicles bearing oil drums would arrive: buses, pickup trucks, taxis. Omar would take a drum, tie it to a rope, and drag it 100 yards across the border to the vehicles waiting on the other side. He might repeat the trip 20 times before daybreak along with hundreds of fellow smugglers, he said. Other men hauled everything from cows to sugar and tea. "It was like a free zone," Omar said.

"Before, now, and in the future, ISIS is smuggling oil into Turkey. And the border guards close their eyes."

If he took in $1,500 in a night, he would give $500 to the FSA commander and another $500 to the Turkish border guards. "You can't really say that we are smuggling oil, because we take permission from the Turkish side and the Syrian side," Omar said. "But since it's under the table, we call it smuggling."

Last fall, ISIS began turn to its attention from fighting the regime to taking territory from fellow rebel groups. As it spread like a parasite within the uprising, it focused on areas rich in oil. By January 2013, it controlled Raqqa, and soon after it was battling for control of the rebel-held parts of Deir Ezzor.

As ISIS gained new oil fields, Omar kept smuggling. He may have worked along an FSA-run border, but he knew he was buying the oil from middlemen who had taken it from ISIS's hands. The trade left a windfall on the Turkish side of the border. "You couldn't step anywhere without stepping in oil," remembered a smuggler in another town near Besaslan, sitting in a dark garage beside three large oil tanks. He was using the money to put himself through trade school. For ISIS, the profits were startup funds as it built up its self-styled caliphate, buying weapons and paying salaries.

Even with U.S. airstrikes now targeting its oil infrastructure, ISIS can make over $1 million a day from the trade, said Luay al-Khatteeb, a visiting fellow at the Brookings Doha Center who directs the Iraq Energy Institute. ISIS controls 60% of the oil-producing resources in eastern Syria, he said, plus a handful of marginal oil fields in Iraq. The group sells most of it within its own territory in Iraq and in Syria—which covers more than 12,000 miles, a size comparable to Belgium, and includes some 8 million people, a population approaching Switzerland's. Desperate residents need the fuel to run their cars, generators, and bakeries.

Khatteeb estimated that even after meeting the demand of local refineries, ISIS still had 30,000 of barrels of oil to export a day, each selling for as much as $35. But its own rudimentary refineries weren't enough to provide for its population, Khatteeb said—so much of the money went toward buying refined oil products from its neighbors, the kind of fuel that can power a taxi or armored Humvee. ISIS makes big profits smuggling oil in Iraq and selling it to the Syrian regime. But Khatteeb called Turkey its most important export market, accounting for "the bulk of the oil trade that ISIS requires to sustain its war machine." ISIS crude oil is exchanged in Turkey for cash, Khatteeb said, or refined fuel.

ISIS surged to global notoriety in June, when it seized the Iraqi city of Mosul. At the same time, it seized 49 Turkish diplomatic staffers and their families from the consulate there. Not long afterward, according to Omar and other sources, the gendarmerie stopped most of the oil-smuggling on the border in Hatay province, where Omar was based. But Omar said it was still easy to work in Besaslan, staying on the Turkish side of the border and taking the oil from the pipes. He believed that the oil still originated in ISIS fields like before.

The pipes extend across the border, where they receive oil from Syrian land controlled by Jabhat al-Nusra, the local branch of al-Qaeda, which was united with ISIS until the two groups split in a power struggle early this year—and has likewise been the target of U.S. airstrikes.

In early October, Omar shot a cell phone video that appears to show another type of smuggling underway. It shows a parade of men carrying oil drums across the border in broad daylight. Omar said he took the video a short drive from Besaslan, on Turkish land, opposite the Syrian border town of Atmeh. The gendarmerie occasionally open the border to let thousands of oil drums enter from Syria in a single night, Omar said. He said the video—which couldn't be verified—shows the tail end of the process: the men walking clusters of emptied drums back across the border and into Syria.

"If I had gotten there earlier, I could have shown you thousands of barrels," Omar said.

Though Omar profited from the oil trade, he said he wanted it to end, and that is why he spoke to BuzzFeed News: It was the worst example of a wartime pillage that has stripped Syria of everything of value, from scrap metal to precious artifacts. "I just want to show the world what they are doing to my country," he said.

A 40-minute drive from Besaslan, the ancient Turkish city of Antakya has crawled with the business of Syria's war since it began. In his sunlit office there, the businessman who claimed that ISIS continues to smuggle oil into Turkey said he'd engaged in similar deals himself. He owned stakes in myriad companies, he said, ranging from energy interests to makers of hair dye. An aging man in black sweatpants and a fleece, he invited his guests to select gifts from a box of hairbrushes that another of his companies made. He said he had purchased oil from both Jabhat al-Nusra and the FSA but not ISIS. "They don't care about the revolution. They just want to earn money," said the businessman, who has been given the pseudonym Yusuf here.

Yusuf said he had bought oil from low-level sellers using makeshift pipelines like the ones in Besaslan. He had also bought it in bulk, he said, receiving oil from Jabhat al-Nusra in trucks that crossed into Turkey at an official border post, with the gendarmerie paid off to let as many as 300 pass in a day. He then sent the oil to a city in Turkey to be refined, he said, though he declined to detail where it went next. "I know the people in Besaslan. They are poor people. They are just carrying the oil and giving it to the buyers, and sometimes they sell it in gas stations here in Turkey," he said. "In other places there are bigger people, and the gendarmerie can protect them."

He added: "The border is like 550 miles, and they are smuggling oil from everywhere," meaning territory held by ISIS and other rebel groups alike.

Sipping coffee in his office, Yusuf produced a contract. He said it showed the kind of oil deals ISIS is pushing for in Turkey now. The contract proposed an agreement between Yusuf, acting on behalf of a Turkish company, and a Syrian middleman acting on behalf of ISIS. It stated that ISIS would sell 3,000 158-liter barrels of oil to the Turkish company each day for a week, for a price of $45 per barrel, and that from there the quantities could increase "when both parties are satisfied."

The contract was unsigned, and Yusuf said he had declined the offer—not because of his dislike of ISIS, he said, but because he didn't like the deal. He asked that his ISIS counterpart not be contacted about the contract—making it impossible to verify. "If you call him about this, he will kill you," Yusuf said, addressing a translator, "he will kill (the journalist), and he will kill me."

But Yusuf did want to work with ISIS in another kind of trade: the ransom of foreign hostages. The freewheeling business of ISIS's oil seemed to attract the same shady characters as the business of its prisoners. European governments have paid multimillion-dollar sums to retrieve their citizens from ISIS's hands—and Yusuf thought that facilitating a deal using his ISIS contacts would net him a sizable commission. From his office, he called the same ISIS middleman listed on the oil contract on his cell phone. "I don't want to do this oil business with you. But I want to work with the journalists," Yusuf said, referring to Western journalists imprisoned by ISIS.

Another businessman based in the Turkish city of Gaziantep also recounted a deep involvement in Syria's illicit oil trade. He'd owned millions of dollars' worth of gas stations, oil refineries and pipelines in Syria—and he had used these resources in oil deals with the FSA. But ISIS commandeered much of this infrastructure early this year, he said. He believed ISIS now used it as part of its sprawling oil trade—and that despite the recent crackdowns, it continued to smuggle oil into Turkey on a large scale. "It's a long border, and there is always a window for something," he said, speaking on condition of anonymity.

Smuggling oil into Turkey was lucrative for ISIS in several ways, the businessman added. It turned profits from the oil it sold, the fees it charged to middlemen, and the taxes it collected at any checkpoints through which the oil passed. "So they are taking money both ways—for wholesale and for transportation," he said.

According to one veteran smuggler who said he brought oil from ISIS territory into Turkey until recently, and who asked to use the nickname Wiyam, the transport fees alone doubled the oil's price by the time he received it at the border. The ISIS militants were deadly serious about the business, he added—and dealing with them almost cost him his life.

When Wiyam began smuggling oil in the Syrian border city of Tel Abyad, before ISIS took control, it was as simple as piping the oil from Syrian trucks into Turkish ones at the official border gate, he said. "It was so easy."

After ISIS took Tel Abyad early this year, Wiyam pledged his allegiance, happy for the chance to work under its name. "Because the ISIS name is terror. It's so powerful," Wiyam said. "But at the same time I was afraid to make any mistakes."

Wiyam later learned that ISIS wanted him to stop his work—because, he believed, it had an oil-smuggling operation of its own. "They have contacts in Turkey," he said. When he and some colleagues continued smuggling in secret anyway, Wiyam said, ISIS caught and executed several of them, and he fled to Turkey.

Soner Cagaptay, the director of the Turkish Research Program at the Washington Institute, said that southern Turkey's long smuggling history is likely to blame for some of the persistence of the illicit oil trade. "You have preexisting smuggling routes that thrive at least in part on corruption, and they have become more active because there's more money involved," he said.

Another factor might be the Turkish government's priorities. While it is opposed to ISIS, it seems more concerned with two other enemies in Syria: the Kurdish militants operating along the border and Syrian President Bashar al-Assad. "The Turks do fear ISIS. They see it as a threat. But their primary objective in Syria remains ousting Assad," Cagaptay said.

An official with the Turkish government, who spoke on condition of anonymity because he wasn't authorized to discuss the matter with the press, said the scale of ISIS's oil trade in the country had been "very much exaggerated." He blamed local corruption for the smuggling that did exist. "This has nothing to do with the state," he said. "The U.S. has big problems on the Mexican border as well. There are problems on any border."

He added: "Assad has been buying ISIS oil for two years now. He has been funding ISIS and Jabhat al-Nusra by buying their oil. And no one says anything about it."

In an emailed statement, officials with the Turkish energy ministry, who declined to be named, said the government "has zero-tolerance for illegal cross-border activities and employs forceful and ongoing measures to prevent oil-smuggling, particularly in the border areas."

The statement added: "Recently, absence of political authority in Syria and parts of Iraq is the main reason of increased smuggling. The rise of [ISIS] has further deteriorated the situation on the Iraqi and Syrian sides of the border. The burden has fallen exclusively on Turkey to confront the smuggling activities."

It acknowledged that the border in southern Turkey had a long history of oil smuggling, but said Turkey has stepped up policing since the outbreak of the Syrian war. The two-page statement detailed additional measures that Turkish authorities had taken to crack down on the smuggling of late. In the first seven months of this year, it said, Turkish authorities had intercepted 5.3 million gallons of smuggled oil along the Syrian and Iraqi borders—a nearly 400% increase from the same period in the previous year. Between Sept. 5–11 alone, it added, Turkish authorities intercepted 3,318 gallons of illicit oil and 7,546 feet of pipe used for smuggling it.

"If there happens [to be] some sort of oil smuggling between the Syrian and Turkish borders, the reason is the challenging task of controlling a border more than [500 miles]," the statement added. It said Turkey regularly exchanged information with the U.S. and other allies on the region's illicit oil trade and that "no intelligence or data has been submitted to Turkish authorities testifying to any kind of involvement of [the] Turkish State and/or officials in cross-border oil smuggling or oil/refined oil products sales or purchase."

If credible evidence emerged that the gendarmerie had turned a blind eye to oil-smuggling, the statement concluded, the government "will definitely take necessary actions to investigate."

A short drive from Besaslan, a stone's throw from Syria, oil drums were stacked against the wall of a cow pen. After traveling to Besaslan and negotiating with the traders there, this is where Omar headed next: one of the black-market filling stops where he brings the oil. This time, he'd agreed to sell it to the owner of the minivan that drove him through Besaslan, a husky 28-year-old Syrian who worked as a driver to support his family living in a refugee camp. The man bought about $50 worth, just enough to fill his tank.

He stuck a piece of hose into a tank the size of a golf cart and began to suck the other end with all his might, using his lungs to get the oil flowing like a human pump.

The driver huffed on the hose for more than 10 minutes as he worked to siphon the oil, swallowing some accidentally from time to time and then stumbling around the cow pens, gasping as oil dripped from his beard.

His mouth on the pipe, he finally got the oil flowing, and he poured it into a rusty can.

He tipped the can into the van's gas tank, then rocked the van furiously to help it go down.

"I have oil right now from here to here," the exhausted driver finally said, pointing from his neck down to his chest.

Omar stood to the side, arms folded behind his back. A herd of cows walked past and into their pens. They were just back from Syria, where farmers took them to feed on the grass—another small part of the pillage. "All things are coming from Syria right now—it's the mother of the world," Omar said. He repeated this several times: "Syria is the mother of the world."

[With additional reporting by Munzer al-Awad and Zaher Said in Turkey.]

What Giglio did with his piece on ISIS, and Winn with his report on the mine in Myanmar, was something they couldn't have done in any printed newspaper. Each is more than 3,500 words. That allowed each story to flourish with color, characters, and details. You'd be hard pressed to find a newspaper editor who would allow such freedom in length for any piece, unless it was a significant exposé. Remember, though, on the web, space is limitless.

However, you'll also notice that both stories are clear and concise. Winn's story even goes farther by using subheads to pace his story. Neither abuses his freedom with space. But, most importantly, each story helps fill the gap in news coverage of the world. On issues and regions that legacy media overlook, new media often step in to invest in the reporting and storytelling needed.

Social Media and Video

The news cycle has long been 24 hours, especially since the advent of cable news. But, since the dawn of social media, the speed of the news cycle has reached a climax. With Twitter, Facebook, Instagram, and Snapchat, news comes from everywhere, all at once. To hitch a ride on the news bullet these days, you must be able to tap into social media.

"Most journalists are expected to be masters of the main social media channels," Knoblich says.

By now, you've already used social media not only in your personal life, but also to help prepare you for your new career as a freelance foreign correspondent. You understand and value its power in journalism. But you must also embrace it on another level as a freelance foreign correspondent operating in the digital space. Still, it poses many challenges for you as a journalist.

There are two strategies for the use of social media as a freelancer foreign correspondent reporting for new media: branding and newsgathering.

Working as an effective reporter for digital media requires you to demonstrate your grasp of social media. To do this, you don't want to just Tweet photos of snacks. Instead, you should regularly share your published content through social media channels, interact with readers, and constantly post supplemental content like short video clips or Periscope live video to enhance your storytelling.

Keep in mind, however, you should match the voice of your social media posts to not only your audience but also to the news organization your piece is for. Your style will vary from pithy to straightforward, depending on what guidance your editors offer you. Yet, you also need to sound authentic to yourself.

"That gets really tricky for reporters particularly if you're working for different outlets," Knoblich says.

But by utilizing social media as a freelance foreign correspondent, you are building your audience and platform while increasing your market value to strings. This also means you're simultaneously strengthening your brand as a journalist capable of navigating and maximizing the use of social media.

Finally, use social media as a tool for newsgathering. You're used to trolling the Facebook and Twitter accounts of news organizations and public figures for news tips and ideas, but you should also tap into the pulse of crowds and news events. For example, if you're covering a large protest or rally, you're unable to survey the entire crowd at once. There may be skirmishes happening two miles from where you are. But, likely, someone somewhere in the crowd is Tweeting about it. While you definitely don't want to report any social media chatter as fact, it should spur you to investigate for your own reporting and verification.

Emerging social media like mobile chat applications also offer promising new opportunities to freelance journalists. WeChat has exploded in places like China. With hundreds of millions of users, chat apps like WeChat offer new frontiers for both storytelling and audience engagement. This is only the beginning of how media use emerging platforms for news.

The other driver of new media content is video. Most editors at digital news organizations would likely tell you that they are seeing a dramatic increase and demand for digital video. Legacy news organizations like the *New York Times* and the *Wall Street Journal* have also invested heavily in video storytelling for the digital world.

Online news organizations are often hungry for any kind of video you can provide to supplement your reporting, according to Cosier: "You can run video shot on an iPhone and email it back in a hurry."

But you can also take more thoughtful and professional approaches to shooting and crafting video, which Cosier often does, when time permits.

Yet, although he often uses professional and costly video newsgathering equipment, his online-only content can be different from the highly edited and self-contained "packages" he'd file for TV broadcasters like the BBC.

"Something that I shoot for broadcast might be slightly different than what I shoot for online," he says. "You can run moments, or just insightful interviews or atmospheric video."

You certainly don't have to invest your life savings in video equipment to take part in the digital video revolution. We discussed earlier in this book about how you should evaluate the expense of professional video newsgathering equipment versus the payoff in jobs. So if you want to gauge your competence, try using the means you already have at your fingertips to experiment with digital video storytelling, like Cosier sometimes does.

Shoot a few clips of video on your smartphone and use a free simple editing program like iMovie to piece together a short video for a story you're already reporting on for a digital news outlet. Submit it to your editor for their thoughts. If they use it, suggest they pay you for your extra work. Remember, most news sites like extra original multimedia content such as video and photos.

This is the simplest way to break into the digital video world, before ensuring you're capable and willing to invest in more professional and efficient video newsgathering equipment.

No matter how seriously you involve yourself in new media as a freelance foreign correspondent, there are some ethical and long-term challenges you should keep in mind, Knoblich says.

For example, how open are you to collaborating on stories that use virtual reality to place users in war zones to illustrate a piece on conflicts in the Middle East? Could you be helping to trigger PTSD in people?

Also, most content online lives forever. So communicate with your editors on who serves as caretakers for your work. Can they update your stories without your approval, days, weeks or years after it's first posted? And, if you do contribute updates to your work, will you get paid for your time?

Even with these challenges, digital media provide boundless reporting opportunities for freelance foreign correspondents. Positioning yourself with the enthusiasm for experimental storytelling and multimedia newsgathering, and plugging yourself into social media allows you to most effectively seize the fast growing potential of this new frontier in journalism.

Notes

1 "How Americans Get their News," March 17, 2014, http://www.americanpressinstitute.org/publications/reports/survey-research/how-americans-get-news/. Accessed October 4, 2015.

2 "News Consumption in the UK: 2014 Report," June, 2014, http://stakeholders.ofcom.org.uk/binaries/research/tv-research/news/2014/News_Report_2014.pdf. Accessed October 4, 2015.

3 Saad, Lydia. "TV is Americans' Main Source of News," July 8, 2013, http://www.gallup.com/poll/163412/americans-main-source-news.aspx. Accessed October 4, 2015.

7

CONFLICT ZONES

There has never been a more dangerous time to be a journalist.

Journalists since war correspondents like Ernest Hemingway and Edward R. Murrow have faced the carnage and chaos of conflicts around the globe. In World War II, 68 foreign correspondents were killed, including legendary Pulitzer Prize-winning newspaper journalist Ernie Pyle.[1] Sixty-six journalists were killed during the bloody Vietnam War.[2] Most of the journalists killed in these 20th century wars died in vehicle or helicopter crashes, friendly fire, mines, or enemy attacks targeting the military convoys in which they were traveling.

But not until the Iraq War did the international journalism profession suffer its bloodiest conflict: Some 150 journalists were killed.[3] The Committee to Protect Journalists marked it as a turning point, saying, "In Iraq, at least 92 journalists, or nearly two out of every three killed, did not die in airstrikes, checkpoint shootings, suicide bombings, sniper fire, or the detonation of improvised explosive devices. They were instead murdered in targeted assassinations in direct reprisal for their reporting."[4]

Now journalists are the prizes for extremists and terrorists. No longer are they valued by militants as conduits for their information. Groups like ISIS have their own information channels: everything from Twitter to YouTube. So journalists are no longer protected, but actually targeted as pawns.

"I felt that 20 years ago in Bosnia, all sides in the war felt they had to trick us or convince us to relay to the world their narrative of the conflict," says Reuters Pulitzer Prize-winning journalist David Rohde. "Today it's open season on journalists."

In 1995 Rohde discovered the mass graves of Srebrenica and was kidnapped by Bosnian Serb forces. Then, 13 years later he, along with several associates, was kidnapped by the Taliban while researching a book in Afghanistan. He was held captive for eight months while the terrorists demanded $25 million for his release. He and a local reporter were finally able to escape.

"Both imprisonments changed my perspective," he says.

Although proud of his past work, Rohde says, for the sake of his family, he no longer covers conflict.

"The tragic circumstance for this is it's more dangerous than ever," Rohde says.

And today, as more news organizations eliminate bureaus and scale back their teams of foreign reporters, they're increasingly relying on freelance foreign war correspondents, many of whom do not have the same support and experience as Rohde did as a reporter for the *New York Times* when he was kidnapped.

"Most of the risks are being run by freelancers,"[5] award-winning American journalist Sebastian Junger told the Huffington Post after he started a group that provides freelancers in war zones emergency medical training. "People really in the meat grinder of the front lines are not, for the most part, insured or salaried network correspondents. They're young freelancers. They're kind of a cheap date for the news industry."

Among the most recent freelance foreign correspondents to die in the line of duty: French photojournalist Camille Lepage who died in the Central African Republic, American journalist Luke Somers who was killed during a failed rescue attempt by U.S. forces to free him from al-Qaeda in Yemen, and Americans Steven Sotloff and James Foley who were executed at the hands of ISIS militants.

Of the more than 1150 journalists killed since 1992 whom CPJ has tracked, the shocking deaths of Sotloff and Foley may have been the most publicized and, possibly, most game-changing.

"It was horrific," says FOX News Jerusalem Correspondent John Huddy. "It was terrible."

Their deaths were more than just gruesome videos shot by merciless killers, but stark signs to the American people of the unique risks freelance journalists face in conflict zones. It exposed the dangers of working independently in high-risk areas.

"A lot of the news organizations welcome their work but told them up front they weren't responsible for safety or any of that," Foley's mother Diane said during a discussion on terrorism and press freedom at the Washington, D.C.-based Newseum in February 2015.[6]

She, like many other Americans, was suddenly exposed to the realities freelance journalists face.

One of several outlets that Foley freelanced for was GlobalPost, and according to his mother Diane, "It was the only one that did step up," when Foley was kidnapped. The news organization even used their insurance to provide a security team to search for Foley.[7]

Sometimes, freelancers' own governments give up on them when they are kidnapped.

"We did not feel Jim was a very high priority," she said. "Our bureaucracy didn't work for us. It didn't work for Jim."[8]

Since her son's death, Diane has worked to advocate for American hostages.

"The American public needs to be aware that this didn't go well," she said.[9]

Her outspoken criticism of the U.S. hostage policy helped prompt President Obama in June 2015 to acknowledge its failures and implement changes, which included the streamlining of communications and oversight in hostage situations of Americans abroad.

She also works to encourage press freedom and education opportunities for disadvantaged children through the James W. Foley Legacy Foundation.

However, Foley's death helped expose to news organizations their shortfalls in their relationships with freelancers.

"[T]he job of reporting from dangerous places has increasingly fallen to eager young freelancers who are paid little and supported—in terms of mentoring, editorial guidance, supplies, etc.—even less," writer Alexis Sobel Fitts reflected in a 2015 article for the *Columbia Journalism Review* entitled "The importance of protecting freelancers."[10]

In response to Foley's death, along with the execution of Sotloff, many news organizations around the world finally joined together to act, protect, and advocate for freelancers.

One of the most meaningful results was the creation of the Global Safety Principles and Practices on February 12, 2015. The alliance of news organizations, freelance reporters and non-profit journalism advocacy groups seeks to increase access to safety and security resources to independent journalists, support them worldwide, and work to better finance their work. Participating organizations include ABC News, CBS News, NBC News, BCC, PBS Frontline, VICE NEWS BuzzFeed, Associated Press,

Agence France-Presse, the Society of Professional Journalists, the Committee to Protect Journalists, and many others.

The initiative takes unprecedented steps to help freelance journalists. News organizations and non-profit journalism advocacy groups involved in the agreement help subsidize conflict reporting safety training, pursue efforts to create a freelancer insurance pool, increase communication channels between freelancers and security directors from U.S. news outlets, and work with American journalism schools to educate students on freelancer training resources.[11]

The alliance commits its editors to treat the welfare of freelance journalists as they do for full-time staffers, pay for their work in a timely manner and ensure they are given fair recognition and credit for their work.[12]

However, at this point the initiative doesn't appear to hold news organizations accountable for paying more of a freelancer's expenses in conflict zones like travel and safety costs, and increasing their pay for assignments to compensate them for the hazards under which they must work. The agreement's language vaguely states news organizations should be more considerate of this.

It does spell out the standards to which journalists on dangerous assignments should adhere themselves. It advises that journalists should have basic skills to properly care for themselves and injured colleagues, have the appropriate protective equipment like helmets and armored jackets, and complete a careful risk assessment and communications strategy prior to the assignment.[13]

These advancements don't necessarily mean freelancers are safe in conflict zones, instead it means they are more prepared, more aware of the risks, and are working with news organizations that are capable of fully supporting them.

The Risks

Even before ISIS executed James Foley and Steven Sotloff, journalists had known they were targets for extremists.

The 2002 videotaped beheading of *Wall Street Journal* South Asia Bureau Chief Daniel Pearl by militants in Pakistan made clear: journalists across the world were fair game.

It had generally been understood that the targeting of journalists was off-limits in war zones. In fact, the Geneva Conventions have long offered some expanded protections to journalists. Most interpretations of the international accord find "journalists are protected under international humanitarian law against direct attacks unless and for such time as they take a direct part in hostilities," according to Robin Geiss, an International Committee of the Red Cross legal expert.[14]

But terrorists are extremists often independent of states. They don't recognize international agreements, and value upending the conventions of the West.

This threat to the safety and security of all journalists in recent years has been felt across the profession.

"I would say the biggest change for me is the concern over security," says Zack Baddorf, a Brooklyn-based freelance journalist who's often reported abroad. "I think there has been a shift in how some militant groups handle and look at journalists."

At the same time, Baddorf says some journalists are acting irresponsibly amid the threat of a murder and kidnapping.

"I think some of them are taking unnecessary risks that are endangering themselves without considering the effects on their loved ones at home," he says.

And to take unnecessary risks like entering war zones without insurance or body armor in the current climate of safety threats to journalists is foolish, at best. Because the inherent nature of war correspondence is too dangerous already.

"I buried too many people in my career who were staff people and freelance people," says Chris Cramer, global head of video for the *Wall Street Journal*, who was taken hostage by gunmen in the Iranian embassy in London while working as a BBC producer in 1980. "I have never felt that that is something responsible news organizations should be encouraging."

Yet, dangerous areas and situations around the world haven't scared off many freelance journalists.

Since the Arab Spring, more freelance journalists are covering conflicts—made possible by cutting-edge mobile technology and low costs, according to Rob Mahoney, deputy director of the Committee to Protect Journalists.

All anyone needs to cover the events unfolding throughout North Africa and the Middle East was a plane ticket, computer, and internet connection. No expensive satellites or high-end video equipment needed.

"The cost of entry into the overseas freelance market has come down remarkably, so there are a lot more people," Mahoney says. "The world has always been dangerous for journalists, but they were fewer in numbers."

The rush of unprepared freelancers to conflict zones ushered in a new world of danger, he says, as these freelance journalists arrive young and inexperienced with fragile relationships to news organizations that might only barely support them. Therefore, more freelancers are putting their safety and security at risk.

Not only that, but the whole idea of what a conflict zone is has changed over the years. No longer is it just a war zone like on the frontlines in Syria and Afghanistan. It could be any place that has the potential to jeopardize your freedom, health, or life. It could be a country suffering from an outbreak of an infectious disease like Ebola, a city exposed to the risk of targeted attacks like Beirut or even Paris, or entire countries like Libya where kidnapping is a regular reality.

And, as a freelancer, the consequences of danger are magnified.

Getting hurt in a conflict zone could mean a costly and dangerous evacuation that jeopardizes the safety of your colleagues, and can leave you with mounting medical bills and years of rehabilitation.

Despite narrowly escaping injury while reporting during riots in Istanbul, I did get hurt while working as a freelancer back home in Baltimore. It's where I was hit in the face and robbed while reporting from a street corner during riots in April 2015 following the controversial death of a black man who died in police custody. I injured my left knee in the attack and went to the hospital that night, before months of rehab and thousands of dollars in medical bills. Had CBS not covered my injury with workers' compensation, it would have made the recovery process that much more difficult. This is a very real possibility for many others freelancers across the world.

Not only are you exposed to physical danger, but mental harm as well, including post-traumatic stress disorder, otherwise referred to as PTSD. Often diagnosed in military combat veterans, its effects include nightmares, flashbacks, difficulty sleeping, anxiety, depression, and suicidal thoughts. It can last for months or years after a traumatic event, and can affect not just veterans but survivors of disasters and, of course, journalists.

One study, according to the U.S. Department of Veterans Affairs, found, "war journalists reported higher weekly alcohol consumption and higher scores on measures of depression and PTSD. The lifetime prevalence rate of PTSD in war journalists was 28.6%, and the lifetime prevalence rate of depression was 21.4%."[15]

Reporting on executions, famine, and mass destruction, all common in conflict zones, can lead to PTSD.

One of the most infamous cases of what might now be diagnosed as PTSD in a journalist was the suicide of photojournalist Kevin Carter in 1994.

The 33-year-old South African had won a Pulitzer Prize just a year before his death for his photograph of a starving toddler collapsed on the ground trying to get to feeding center being stalked by a vulture during a famine in the Sudan. Although he had long been exposed to the horrors of apartheid, according to his *New York Times* obituary, he later told an interviewer after he shot the Sudan photo "he sat under a tree for a long time, 'smoking cigarettes and crying.'"[16]

But for a long time, journalists who'd reported from conflict zones never acknowledged their emotional and mental health issues.

"There was a stigma attached to it," says Cramer. "I never went to see a shrink."

Cramer admits, "For a significant period of time I was a basket case."

To compound the effects of PTSD, many journalists would return home after assignments without the support from their news organizations or even their own families.

"Some foreign correspondents have struggled to maintain marriages and families," says Huddy.

Rohde had a similar experience facing PTSD, although he says his employer the *New York Times* was very supportive and helped get him counseling.

The counseling "helps me be a better reporter, colleague, and person," Rohde says.

Today, it's more common for news organizations to help their journalists get the care they need to address emotional and mental health issues.

"It's being talked about a lot at the moment," says Balint Szlanko, a freelance foreign correspondent based in Hungary but accustomed to working in war zones. "I don't think it was a few years ago."

Aside from seeking emotional and mental health resources, many correspondents in conflict zones like Huddy rely on short breaks.

"You need to take breaks," he says. "It's good to go back home and to just take time off."

So if you're considering reporting from any conflict zone are you prepared to suffer similar challenges? How will you get the help you need if you need it? Who will pay for it? And have you discussed this with the news organizations you'll be working for to ensure you have their support?

Beyond just the risk of getting hurt or suffering from PTSD, journalists in conflict zones also face unique challenges from kidnapping and death.

Both scenarios will have devastating effects on your loved ones. It will also be a burden for your government as it tries to secure your release or the repatriation of your body.

Costs

It's true: Getting to and reporting from conflict zones is much more affordable than it was years ago. But doing it properly and responsibly will still cost you heavily as a freelance foreign correspondent.

"I think it's more expensive than ever to report safely," says Rohde.

It's not just the costly protective equipment you'll need to have with you in conflict areas, but the ancillary costs that can really push you to your financial limits.

To effectively report from dangerous locations, you'll need to rely on drivers, fixers, and translators. You might also need to bring with you days' worth of supplies like food and clean water and have a way to transport it all safely and securely, which might include several vehicles, according to BBC Producer Simon Hughes. Even finding electricity might be a challenge.

War reporting "requires a massive amount of self-reliance," Hughes says. And "it's not cheap."

At the same time you're competing against many others for the same resources.

"All the large organizations are going to hire up the best local journalists," says Rohde. "Freelancers with few resources can find themselves at a disadvantage."

Television networks and large news organizations with the budgets to match will only drive up the costs of hiring key people to help you with your reporting. Supply and demand will be just one more of your enemies.

"People complain when a story breaks and TV channels show up, prices go up," says Szlanko.

A driver who knows his way around who might cost $50 in Istanbul for the entire day, could cost several hundred dollars if you're competing with full-time staffers from large news organizations that can guarantee many days of work for him. The sheer hazards of working in a war zone will add to the costs of recruiting local hires to work in dangerous conditions.

The same financial consideration must be given to your accommodations. If at all possible, it's best to stay in a large protected hotel with in-house security. Besides offering basic conveniences and a relatively safe live shot and filing location, it offers you protection from being kidnapped. Remember, you're a valuable target. Staying in an unprotected hotel or home could expose you to dangerous situations. However, the large hotels will be costly. Each night will add up.

Sometimes, you'll also need your own armed personal protection. Imagine if you're a foreign journalist with an expensive computer, mobile phone, photography, or video equipment. You're valuable not only for what you own but who you are. Many news organizations, especially TV networks, will only travel to especially dangerous war zones with a team of security contractors, and often in armored vehicles.

If the threat of death, kidnapping, injury, or financial insolvency hasn't scared you off yet, then make sure you take every step possible to prepare for your work seriously and responsibly.

Preparation

Freelance journalists who are determined to report from conflict zones have much more preparation to do beforehand. Besides reviewing the Global Safety Principles and Practices, they should also work with their strings to strategize their coverage plans.

Before you commit to accepting the responsibilities associated with dangerous assignments, ensure you are first properly trained.

Elisabet Cantenys, Head of Programmes for the non-profit UK-based freelance journalist assistance group Rory Peck Trust, says it's essential that freelancers are taught first aid and safety skills for the protection of themselves and their colleagues.

In a conflict zone, "sooner or later something will happen to you," Cantenys says.

News organizations, security companies and non-profit groups offer hazardous situation safety courses at locations around the world. But Cantenys recommends you carefully evaluate these hostile environment training programs and the instructors before signing up.

Among the first considerations: the length of the course.

"I honestly think anything less than three days is not sufficient," she says. "You can't do a shortcut."

Next, look at the curriculum. It should be tailored to meet the specific needs of freelance journalists, not military contractors or other groups in conflict zones, she says. It should definitely include security threat evaluation and first aid training.

Ensure that the course has a track record of training other journalists, and that the instructors are experienced.

There should also be space available to practice conflict zone scenarios and first aid procedures, according to Cantenys.

Non-profit organizations like the Rory Peck Trust offer guidance on what programs are available and can verify the quality of their training. Some are as long as five days, and include certifications for skills like first aid. They can be costly at several hundred dollars or even thousands if travel and insurance are necessary. However, RPT, along with a few other journalism advocacy organizations, offers limited funds to help subsidize the costs.

Highly regarded hostile environment training programs include those offered by Reporters Instructed in Saving Colleagues with courses in the U.S., Europe, and Africa; Washington, D.C.-based Global Journalist Security with another training center in Nairobi, Kenya; and, London-based 1st Option High Risk.

Increasingly, some news organizations are refusing to work with freelancers in conflict zones who have *not* completed these training programs.

Additionally, you'll need to complete a risk assessment form (one provided by Rory Peck Trust is included as Appendix B). You can find detailed instructions on RoryPeckTrust.org. It should include an outline of your assignment, the location, a detailed list of all possible risks you might face there, emergency health and evacuation plans, insurance information, protective equipment and documentation, and information on your accommodations. You should share this with the news organizations you'll be working with.

"It's something that should be for everybody," in any situation where safety and security could be a concern—even in a rally in London that could turn violent, according to Cantenys.

Along with the risk assessment form, a communication plan (Appendix C, courtesy of RPT) should also be completed. It should list your key safety contacts and how often and through what methods you'll be regularly in touch with them. It will also include what emergency preparations will be activated if you fail to make regular contact with them. The plan will also state a "communications code" that will be used to alert someone included in the plan if communications are being monitored or compromised.

You should also share with your contacts four questions and their answers known only to you and those close to you, to be used to verify if you are alive if you are taken hostage or detained.

I also recommend going a step further by creating a will and instructions on what you want done with your body if you die abroad.

Share these documents with your loved ones, and the news organizations you'll be working with during your dangerous assignment.

Finally, depending on what risks you've evaluated you'll want to locate the appropriate protective equipment such as the armored vests called "flak jackets," helmets, and gas masks. These can easily cost hundreds of dollars each, so some freelancers choose to cut corners by borrowing or sharing them, or buying or renting second-hand equipment instead of purchasing them new.

But, Cantenys warns, you should always know the history of the protective equipment you are using. Has it been damaged? How old is it? What uses has the equipment been exposed to?

It should also fit properly, because if it doesn't or if it's damaged, it's useless to you.

"If you don't have the right safety equipment, you may be better not having any," Cantenys says.

It can be costly to ship this heavy equipment, so Cantenys explains that freelancers can rent them on location, if possible.

But remember, "you need to trust the people renting them" to you, Cantenys says.

Choosing to rent or buy quality protective equipment will be expensive, but Cantenys says, "this is your life, it's worth investing in."

You should also evaluate how your digital and communications equipment might expose you to security risks. What data do you have that might be of interest to adversaries? Can they use any of your communications equipment to track your location? How can you securely send and receive information anonymously or securely? And how restrictive and current are your privacy and encryption settings on your mobile devices, computer, and even social media? Additional information on this can be found on RoryPeckTrust.org.

The risks that freelance journalists expose themselves to in conflict zones are extreme. Yet, as Rohde notes, "Many journalists have made their names" in war correspondence in what is "the longest tradition in journalism," dating back to the Civil War in the U.S.

The adrenaline from the coverage of conflicts can also be addictive for some.

"It's a rush," Huddy says. "That's how my personality is."

War correspondence also means you're around a unique fraternity of fellow journalists with experiences only they can share.

"I think there is a shared personality in a sense that I think you have to have," Huddy says.

But before beginning your work in this dangerous type of journalism, you must weigh whether the personal gratification of telling these important stories is still ultimately worth both your life and sanity.

"You don't have to make your name as a conflict reporter," Rohde says. The profession needs new generations of business, political, and other types of reporter.

In fact, if there's one idea to take away from this book it's that the majority of foreign correspondents are not war correspondents. But that's difficult to imagine when every night on the news viewers see foreign reporters on the frontlines of wars around the globe. Yet these reporters are actually in the minority. Pages and pages of newspapers and websites, and many hours of other broadcasts, are filled with stories from journalists far from conflicts.

You might risk your savings on telling and selling foreign news, but you certainly don't have to risk your life.

Working as a foreign correspondent, no matter how many challenges you face in a strange country thousands of miles from home, is life and career changing. There has never been a more accessible time to be a freelance foreign correspondent. With the right preparation, the world can be in the palm of your hand and the pages of your notebook.

Notes

1 Smyth, Frank. "Iraq War and News Media: A Look inside the Death Toll," Committee to Protect Journalists, March 2003, https://cpj.org/blog/2013/03/iraq-war-and-news-media-a-look-inside-the-death-to.php. Accessed November 13, 2015.

2 Smyth.

3 Smyth.

4 Smyth.

5 Calderone, Michael. "Sebastian Junger Launches Medical Training Program for Freelance Journalists in War Zones," *Huffington Post*, March 20, 2012, http://www.huffingtonpost.com/2012/03/20/sebastian-junger-risc-freelance-journalists-tim-hetherington_n_1367429.html. Accessed November 15, 2015.

6 "Terrorism and Press Freedom: Mothers, Journalists Speak Out," Newseum, February 5, 2013, http://www.newseum.org/2015/02/05/terrorism-and-press-freedom-mothers-journalists-speak-out/#sthash.wgB7bD6T.dpuf. Accessed November 13, 2015.

7 Newseum.

8 Newseum.

9 Newseum.

10 Sobel Fitts, Alexis. "The Importance of Protecting Freelancers," *Columbia Journalism Review*, January/February 2015, http://www.cjr.org/feature/protecting_freelancers.php. Accessed November 15, 2015.

11 "Sotloff Fdn, Four U.S. TV Networks Sign onto Safety Principles," October 5, 2015, http://dartcenter.org/content/sotloff-foundation-and-four-us-television-networks-sign-onto-safety-principles#.VkjKCsrDlJ8. Accessed November 15, 2015.

12 "Global Safety Principles and Practices," February 12, 2015, http://dartcenter.org/content/global-safety-principles-and-practices#.VkjJkcrDlJ8. Accessed November 15, 2015.

13 "Global Safety Principles and Practices."

14 "How does International Humanitarian Law Protect Journalists in Armed-conflict Situations?" July 27, 2010, https://www.icrc.org/eng/resources/documents/interview/protection-journalists-interview-270710.htm. Accessed November 15, 2015.

15 Bolton, PhD, Elisa E. "Journalists and PTSD," PTSD: National Center for PTSD. August 15, 2015, http://www.ptsd.va.gov/public/community/journalists-ptsd.asp. Accessed November 15, 2015.

16 Keller, Bill. "Kevin Carter, a Pulitzer Winner For Sudan Photo, is Dead at 33." *New York Times*, July 29, 1994, http://www.nytimes.com/1994/07/29/world/kevin-carter-a-pulitzer-winner-for-sudan-photo-is-dead-at-33.html. Accessed November 15, 2015.

APPENDIX A

Jane Doe, Istanbul, Turkey

Client:	Buzzfeed		Invoice #: 002–2016	Invoice Date: 30/2/2016
DATE FILED	**CONTENT**	**EDITOR**	**LOCATION**	**FEE $USD**
2/7/2016	"Skiing the Balkans"	Kim Dawson	Kopaonik, Serbia	$ 300.00
2/20/2016	"Turkey Cracks Down on Social Media"	Michael Newman	Ankara, Turkey	$ 350.00
2/26/2016	"Protests Rock Istanbul"	Kim Dawson	Istanbul, Turkey	$ 290.00
			TOTAL DUE	USD $940.00

Jane Doe
Camadan Sk. No. 55,
Daire: 2
Çatma Mescit, 34430
Beyoğlu/İstanbul, Turkey
US: +1 555 410 5875
TK: +90 312 555 7766
jdoe@janedoereports.com

Chemical Bank
Routing # 123456789
Account # 9876543210

All payments are due within 30 days of receipt of invoice.
Late fees will apply.

APPENDIX B

Confidential—Guidance only

Reprinted with Permission. © Rory Peck Trust www.rorypecktrust.org

Date of Risk Assessment

COUNTRY: Name
DATES OF TRAVEL/ASSIGNMENT: Dates

[*Refer to Risk Assessment Notes 1 on our site for the following*]

ASSIGNMENT OUTLINE: Include a travel plan, interviews, story outline.

LOCATIONS AND BRIEF SCHEDULE
Provide your information here.

ASSIGNMENT DETAILS (Give specific details of what you intend to cover to complete your assignment)
Provide your information here.

PROJECT SPECIFIC RISKS (Name and describe main risks)

1) Are you working on a sensitive topic? Yes/No. What is it, and why is it sensitive?

2) Are you covering a high risk location, activity or event? Yes/no. Describe the location, activity or event.

3) Who will you be meeting, are they potentially under surveillance, and might they be at risk if they talk to you?

4) Is your security threatened by talking to specific people, visiting or working in a specific area?

Circle or underline any of the following risks you may face:

abduction/kidnapping, violent and organized crime, abusive state security forces, corruption (bribery), riots/demonstrations, armed conflict, terrorist attack, road side bombs/IEDS/body traps, landmines and unexploded ordinance (UXO), low intensity warfare/guerrilla war, cultural hostility, petty crime/theft, car-jacking, road accidents and other transport (aircraft, boat), crossing borders/checkpoints, political instability, outbreak of hostilities, death squads, militia, gangs, natural disaster (flood, earthquake), extreme weather, environmental hazards/toxins/poisons, physical and/or electronic surveillance, infectious diseases.

Details on risks you may face: Create as many entries as you need. Each should cover the following:

1) Name and describe the risk
    a. How serious is it? Not very/Somewhat/Extremely serious
    b. How likely is it? Not very/Somewhat/Extremely likely
    c. What measures are you taking to reduce the chance and severity?

2) Name and describe the risk
    a. How serious is it? Not very/Somewhat/Extremely serious
    b. How likely is it? Not very/Somewhat/Extremely likely
    c. What measures are you taking to reduce the chance and severity?

3) Name and describe the risk
    a. How serious is it? Not very/Somewhat/Extremely serious
    b. How likely is it? Not very/Somewhat/Extremely likely
    c. What measures are you taking to reduce the chance and severity?

4) Name and describe the risk
    a. How serious is it? Not very/Somewhat/Extremely serious
    b. How likely is it? Not very/Somewhat/Extremely likely
    c. What measures are you taking to reduce the chance and severity?

5) Name and describe the risk
    a. How serious is it? Not very/Somewhat/Extremely serious
    b. How likely is it? Not very/Somewhat/Extremely likely
    c. What measures are you taking to reduce the chance and severity?

Continue adding as many risks as you can think of in this format.

[*Refer to* _Risk Assessment Notes 2_ *on our site for the following*]

PASSPORT, VISAS, PRESS ACCREDITATION AND COVER STORY
Passport
Passport number:
Date of issue:
Expiring date:
Country of issue/Nationality:

Visa information
Provide details here, and attach relevant documents and correspondence to this document.

Press accreditation and/or cover story
How will you obtain this?

If you are travelling undercover or as a tourist, give details of your cover story.

TRAVEL RISKS: What are the risks involved in your travel arrangements?

1) Name and describe the travel risk
   a. How serious is it? Not very/Somewhat/Extremely serious
   b. How likely is it? Not very/Somewhat/Extremely likely
   c. What measures are you taking to reduce the chance and severity?

2) Name and describe the travel risk
   a. How serious is it? Not very/Somewhat/Extremely serious
   b. How likely is it? Not very/Somewhat/Extremely likely
   c. What measures are you taking to reduce the chance and severity?

3) Name and describe the travel risk
   a. How serious is it? Not very/Somewhat/Extremely serious
   b. How likely is it? Not very/Somewhat/Extremely likely
   c. What measures are you taking to reduce the chance and severity?

Continue adding as many risks as you can think of in this format.

HEALTH AND MEDICAL

1. Do you need to take any vaccinations?
   a. Which vaccines do you need?
   b. What are the risks in not having them?
   c. Where have you got/will you get them?

You may want to attach copies of any vaccine files to this document.

2. Do you (or does anyone else on your team, if relevant) have any medical condition that you and others need to take into account and/or pose a risk? List each medical condition:
   a. What are the risks of travelling with each medical condition?
   b. How severe are the risks?
   c. How likely is it?
   d. What are you doing to reduce the chance and severity of the risk?

3. List any prescription medication you must take:
   a. Medication name:
   b. Dosage amount and frequency:

List as many items as necessary here in similar fashion. You may want to attach copies of prescription information or related medical details to this document.

4. Would you have access to a hospital with international standards?
    a. How far and how difficult it would be for you to reach this hospital?

5. How will you be evacuated in an emergency?
    a. From where to where, by whom and at what cost?
    b. Does your insurance provide cover for this?

INSURANCE

Do you have insurance that covers you while on assignment? Yes/No

What kind(s) of insurance cover to you have? Give the policy name and a description here for each:

Who is/are the insurance provider(s)? For each, give the provider's name, address and contact details here:

Give details about what each insurance policy covers:

You may want to attach copies of relevant insurance papers to this document. It may be helpful to consult the Insurance resource at www.rorypecktrust.org.

[Refer to Risk Assessment Notes 3 on our site for the following]

PROFILE RISKS: Is there an increased risk as a result of your gender, age, ethnicity, religious beliefs or nationality? How about those accompanying you?

1. Name and describe the travel risk
    a. How serious is it? Not very/Somewhat/Extremely serious
    b. How likely is it? Not very/Somewhat/Extremely likely
    c. What measures are you taking to reduce the chance and severity?

2. Name and describe the travel risk
    a. How serious is it? Not very/Somewhat/Extremely serious
    b. How likely is it? Not very/Somewhat/Extremely likely
    c. What measures are you taking to reduce the chance and severity?

Continue adding as many risks as you can think of in this format.

FIXERS AND OTHER LOCALLY HIRED FREELANCERS

1. What are the risks related to your locally hired professional support?

2. What are the credentials and experience of local fixer/driver/translator that make them suitable for this assignment?

3.   Name and describe another risk in this area
   a.   How serious is it? Not very/Somewhat/Extremely serious
   b.   How likely is it? Not very/Somewhat/Extremely likely
   c.   What measures are you taking to reduce the chance and severity?

Continue adding as many risks as you can think of in this format.

EQUIPMENT AND CARNET

What professional kit are you taking with you? List it here. (Consider and adapt to your specific needs and potential risks)

What are the import regulations/restrictions in your destination country? List them here.

Do you require a carnet?

Provide a detailed equipment list with serial numbers here:

1.   Item
   a.   Make and model:
   b.   Serial number:

2.   Item
   a.   Make and model:
   b.   Serial number:

3.   Item
   a.   Make and model:
   b.   Serial number:

Continue adding as many risks as you can think of in this format.

Consider attaching relevant equipment receipts or other information to this document.

What are the risks related to the equipment you need to take?

1.   Name and describe the risk
   a.   How serious is it? Not very/Somewhat/Extremely serious
   b.   How likely is it? Not very/Somewhat/Extremely likely
   c.   What measures are you taking to reduce the chance and severity?

2.   Name and describe the risk
   a.   How serious is it? Not very/Somewhat/Extremely serious
   b.   How likely is it? Not very/Somewhat/Extremely likely
   c.   What measures are you taking to reduce the chance and severity?

3.   Name and describe the risk
   a.   How serious is it? Not very/Somewhat/Extremely serious
   b.   How likely is it? Not very/Somewhat/Extremely likely
   c.   What measures are you taking to reduce the chance and severity?

Continue adding as many risks as you can think of in this format.

PERSONAL PROTECTION EQUIPMENT

1. What safety equipment do you need? (flak jacket, tear gas goggles, helmet, etc.)

2. How will you obtain it?

3. Can you get this equipment to the location? How will you do so?

4. What is the risk of travelling with this equipment?
    a. How likely is it that a problem will arise? Not very/Somewhat/Extremely likely
    b. What measures are you taking to reduce the chance and severity?

5. What is the risk of obtaining this equipment at the location?
    a. How likely is it that a problem will arise? Not very/Somewhat/Extremely likely
    b. What measures are you taking to reduce the chance and severity?

List any other risks here in a similar fashion.

RUSHES/RECORDINGS/NOTES AND MATERIALS

1. How will you store information and/or your material?
    a. What are the risks in doing this?
    b. How likely are the risks?
    c. What measures are you taking to reduce the chances and severity of the risks?

2. Would loss or confiscation put you or other people at risk?
    a. How likely is this risk?
    b. What measures are you taking to reduce the chances and severity?

3. How will you get your material out of the country/location?
    a. What are the risks in doing this?
    b. How likely are the risks?
    c. What measures are you taking to reduce the chances and severity of the risks?

4. What data-wrangling and back-up regime will you be operating?
    a. What could go wrong?
    b. How likely are the risks?
    c. What measures are you taking to reduce the chances and severity of the risks?

ACCOMMODATION

What are the main risks related to your lodging(s)?

1. Name and describe the risk
    a. How likely would the risk be?
    b. How serious would the risk be?
    c. What measures are you taking to reduce the chances and severity of the risk?

2. Name and describe the risk
   a. How likely would the risk be?
   b. How serious would the risk be?
   c. What measures are you taking to reduce the chances and severity of the risk?

3. Name and describe the risk
   a. How likely would the risk be?
   b. How serious would the risk be?
   c. What measures are you taking to reduce the chances and severity of the risk?

List any other risks here in a similar fashion.

A checklist about your lodgings. Answer the following:

1. Are there already some security measures in place (e.g. guards)?

2. Who else is staying there (e.g. diplomats, other journalists, tourists)?

3. How close are you to potential terrorist targets (e.g. embassies, tourist destination, barracks, etc.)?

4. How might your accommodation affect your profile?

5. How easy would access and egress be in the event of an emergency?

6. How able is the building to withstand attack, do you need to tape the windows, is there a basement?

7. Does the building, area, have a history of problems/incidents?

COMMUNICATIONS
This section will be helped by completing your Communications Plan.

How will you communicate with your safety contacts, sources, colleagues and others? Email? Mobile? Land line phone? Postal system? Voice over internet or online chatting? Filesharing?

Could any of these methods be compromised or compromise your safety and/or that of others?

Go through your communication methods below:

1. Type of communication
   a. The potential risks of this method
   b. The likelihood of this risk happening. Not likely/Somewhat/Extremely likely
   c. The severity of this risk. Not very/Somewhat/Extremely severe
   d. What steps are you taking to reduce the chance and severity of the risk?

2. Type of communication
    a. The potential risks of this method
    b. The likelihood of this risk happening. Not likely/Somewhat/Extremely likely
    c. The severity of this risk. Not very/Somewhat/Extremely severe
    d. What steps are you taking to reduce the chance and severity of the risk?

3. Type of communication
    a. The potential risks of this method
    b. The likelihood of this risk happening. Not likely/Somewhat/Extremely likely
    c. The severity of this risk. Not very/Somewhat/Extremely severe
    d. What steps are you taking to reduce the chance and severity of the risk?

List as many items as you need here similar fashion.

You may want to refer to the Digital Security resource at www.rorypecktrust.org for ideas.

How will you be able to reassess your main risks while on assignment?
Include here how you plan to assess changes in the situation and communicate them to your safety contact(s).

CLOSING
This document and all its attached files should accompany your Communications Plan and Proof of Life documents. These should be kept with reliable contacts who will be available to you and will have your contact details.

The Risk Assessment, Communications Plan and Proof of Life Questions are the key documents for your **Emergency File**, a folder that contains important personal safety information like copies of your passport and visa and a copy of your vaccination book. Your Risk Assessment will also contain personal information such as your blood type and any other relevant medical information like allergies and medical conditions, insurance policy details, flight details and your itinerary/schedule.

APPENDIX C

Confidential—NOT FOR TRAVEL

Reprinted with Permission. © Rory Peck Trust www.rorypecktrust.org

Date goes here

This is the communications plan for staying in communication with your key safety contact(s). You and your contacts should agree to the information you've provided here and stick with it.

How often do you need to be in touch with your key contact?
Through what methods? (Be as specific as possible)

Failure to do so:
1)
2)
3)
4)
5)
etc.

Failure to make contact and confirm you and your team are fine will result in emergency preparations being considered, after **XX** hours, and activated, after **xx** hours.

Emergency Communications Plan:
1)
2)
3)
4)
5)
etc.

Emergency Contacts List:
Name
Role/Relationship
Contact details
Location
Time zone
Phone number (include dialling code and language instructions)

Name
Role/Relationship
Contact details
Location
Time zone
Phone number (include dialling code and language instructions)

Create as many of these as you need in this format

PERSONNEL DETAILS
(Form needs to accommodate one set for each person on location)

Name	Position
Mobile phone	Home phone number
Address	
Email	Skype
DoB	Blood group

Personal circumstances and dependants
Name of partner (with details)
Next of kin (with details)
Brief biography (credentials and why are this person is suitable for this assignment)

If you're travelling with others, create this for each person.

Itinerary/Schedule
Give details of travel, vehicles and departure and arrival times, routes and anything else necessary.

Communications Code
If communications are monitored or compromised, come up with a pass code that will alert the other person. Create pass codes for different kinds of information that you may need to communicate.

INDEX